POPULATING
CLAY LANDSCAPES

POPULATING CLAY LANDSCAPES

JESSICA MILLS AND ROG PALMER

TEMPUS

First published 2007

Tempus Publishing Limited
The Mill, Brimscombe Port,
Stroud, Gloucestershire, GL5 2QG
www.tempus-publishing.com

British Library Cataloguing in Publication Data.
A catalogue record for this book is available from the British Library.

ISBN 978 0 7524 4093 4

Typesetting and origination by Tempus Publishing Limited
Printed in Great Britain

Contents

III Results

Endpiece

Introduction

Jessica Mills and Rog Palmer

INTRODUCTION

This book brings together, for the first time, a number of key investigations and insights into the settlement of clay landscapes. Clay soils and geologies make up significant areas of Britain and Europe; however, until recently little archaeological investigation has been undertaken on such formations.

Indeed, clay soils and geologies have long been problematical for archaeologists, aerial photographers and archaeological surveyors. They are usually characterised as poor and heavy soils which, when wet, are regularly waterlogged and in dry periods can become like concrete. Such characteristics have, over the years, led many to think of clay landscapes as unsuitable places for past settlement and agriculture. This pessimistic view of clay has dominated archaeological narratives biasing interpretations of land use and settlement. With clay being perceived in such a negative light, the number of archaeological investigations on the claylands has been minimal compared with that on other soils (1). This is compounded by the fact that over the past few decades most developer-led archaeological projects have been undertaken within the densely populated river valleys of Britain and Europe.

With few archaeological surveys being conducted on clay environs, few sites are ever discovered, which re-affirms the view that claylands were unpopular landscapes in the past. This attitude towards clay has prevailed for many years and is only now beginning to be challenged by the increasing number of archaeological interventions upon clay landscapes. With the progressive development of green-field sites outside of river valleys, as well as landscape-wide development schemes such as roads and pipelines,

Left: 1 Fieldwork on clay? These boots may suggest why so few archaeologists have been attracted to working on clay landscapes. © *Kath Mills*

Opposite: 2 Excavations by Albion Archaeology in advance of the A428 Caxton Common to Hardwick improvement. Site 5 is on high ground and was continually occupied from the second century to the ladder settlement, which continued in use to the end of the Roman period. © *Rog Palmer: 20051027-085, 27 October 2005*

the opportunities for archaeologists to examine clay landscapes are rapidly growing. With this upturn in archaeological investigations it becomes even more important that we, as archaeologists, re-examine our attitudes towards clay. Not surprisingly, the more investigations that are carried out on clay soils and geologies, the more archaeology is found. As will be shown from the contributions in this book, the claylands of Britain and Europe were extensively utilised landscapes in the past, and through current ground and aerial archaeological surveys we are only seeing the tip of the iceberg.

POPULATING THE CLAY

From Masters research work looking at aerial photographs in the largely clay county of Bedfordshire (JM) to a lifetime of mapping archaeological features on the 'difficult' soils of the East Midlands/East Anglia (RP), the editors have long been aware that clay geologies and soils are not as poor as they are often made out to be. Indeed, having spent many years living and working in the clay region around Bedford and Cambridge, we have seen how the claylands form a fundamental facet of local identity. From being the core component of the famous brick-making industries at Stewartby, south of Bedford and around Peterborough, to dictating the types of agricultural activity that can be undertaken, clay landscapes are, and were, a constituent part of many communities.

It is from such a backdrop that the editors were inspired to organise a one-day conference at the University of Leicester in November 2005 to bring together people who had been involved with archaeological investigations on clay soils and geologies. The conference attracted a cross-section of interested parties ranging from archaeological field units, national and local government heritage departments, universities and the

general public. The majority of the papers presented at the conference are disseminated here – and it is hoped that through doing so a greater awareness of the past settlement and use of the claylands is elicited.

INVESTIGATING THE CLAY

Aerial survey

Archaeological aerial survey has recorded extensive landscapes and numerous individual features on river gravels and chalkland. These rich and densely occupied areas have made such places easy targets for academic research resulting in a plethora of syntheses on those bedrocks (e.g. Allen 1938; 1940; Webster and Hobley 1965; Benson and Miles 1974; Palmer 1984; Fulford and Nichols 1992; Stoertz 1997). However, these areas constitute only a small part of Britain and Europe, and surveys that fail to include a more representative spectrum of geology will provide a partial and biased view of our past.

The claylands in Britain have a long history of being considered a blank area for pre-medieval settlement and it has proven difficult for archaeological aerial photographers to come to terms with. In his book *Ancient Landscapes*, John Bradford wrote it off in a sentence, 'But clay soils are very rarely of any use.' (1957, 15) and most airborne photographers tended to glance at it in passing while heading for the soils they knew to be more prolific in information. There seemed to be a belief that all types of clay were equally bad although one slightly puzzled sentence was written by the aerial photographer, Derrick Riley, 'It is difficult to comment on crop marks on clay, because although they are usually rare on this material, they are common on clayey soils in the Lincolnshire Fens' (Riley 1987, 35-7). Of all the aerial photographers active at that time, Riley undertook the most investigation into what he called 'cropmarkology' – the reasons why and how crops grew differently above sub-surface features. Riley's confusion is likely to have been due only to the fact that both deposits are named 'clay' although, by the time Riley was writing, it was known that the inland clays (the subject of this book) were an entirely different form of deposit to the Fen clays. The latter were initially marine deposits that later became dry ground that was intensively occupied during the Roman period (Phillips 1970). Away from the Fenland, recent investigations are tending to show that all inland clay deposits should not be considered the same (see Mills 2003; 2005 and Evans, this volume). So not only are we now able to recognise considerable past activity on clays but, within 'the clay', different deposits appear to have been used differently in the past.

In England there has been some attention paid to claylands by archaeological aerial photographers since the 1970s. Notably, Jim Pickering and Glenn Foard were persistent enough to fly regularly over these supposedly barren landscapes in Leicestershire and Northamptonshire. Foard's work has formed a vital component of the Northamptonshire National Mapping Programme and is summarised by Deegan in this volume. A more-localised aerial survey by Chris Cox in west Cambridgeshire first identified many of the sites that were later excavated in advance of building the new village of Cambourne and along the A428 trunk road (2, 3; see also Abrams and Ingham forthcoming). There has yet to be published a detailed comparison of what was visible from the air in these locations and what was found on the ground.

The breakthrough that proved certain clays to be as densely packed with archaeological sites as were the lighter soils was the series of vertical photographs taken of Bedfordshire in 1996 – and it was these that led to the idea of a book on clayland archaeology. Stephen Coleman (this volume) comments about the acquisition of such photographs. Such surveys are a recurrent event over most English counties but the archaeological potential of such complete photographic cover can be maximised if an appropriate time of year can be chosen for its flying. On the basis of rapid examination of a 300sq km area of the Bedfordshire 1996 survey there were likely to be some 1200 archaeological sites recorded in a few hours throughout the county. There is no way that this number of sites, even within a comparatively small area, could be photographed using archaeology's preferred observer-directed survey which takes site-centred oblique photographs and it seems high time that we sought alternative methods of photographing the ground (Palmer 2005).

The site-orientated oblique photography also implies that archaeologists are interested only in the sites themselves (Mills 2005). This is clearly not the case and most modern landscape or site-centred studies require environmental information of the type that can be well-recorded from the air. Palaeochannels (relict watercourses), for example, are bands of deeper soil and so affect crop growth at the same time as do buried archaeological ditches and pits. While these occur more usually in fluvial landscapes such as floodplains, there are some natural features that occur on clay soils. These include slades and areas of tertiary deposit which may have had crucial roles to play in the locations and design of

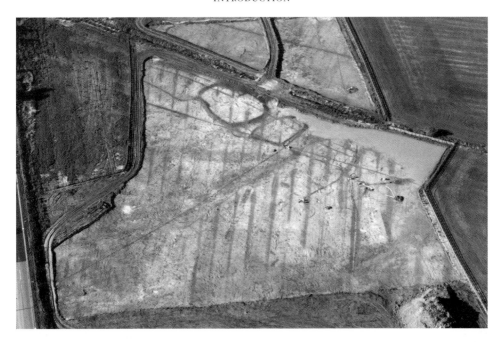

3 Excavations by Albion Archaeology in advance of the A428 Caxton Common to Hardwick improvement. Site 7 is a farmstead consisting of three main enclosures, some with associated paddocks. Occupation began with a mid-Iron Age farmstead that later developed through an additional two phases. Analysis of faunal remains (sheep, cattle), molluscan species and the results of a geo-archaeological survey show the site was in open grassland. © *Rog Palmer: 20051027-092, 27 October 2005*

past settlements, land allotment and communications. Hence recording such information is imperative to the better understanding of how people interacted with the land.

Aerial survey and observation that has been done over clay landscapes has shown that crops develop over archaeological sites at a later date than they do on 'easier' soils. Thus, any aerial observation over the clays during the usual 'crop-mark season' would be unlikely to identify anything worthy of photography. This is confirmed to some extent by the absence of information on clay soils on long flights made during this time (such as made by Cambridge University and English Heritage working from airfields at Cambridge and Oxford respectively) that transit over claylands to reach their preferred survey areas. This comment is, of course, based on the assumption that an archaeological observer will keep constantly assessing the ground during any flight.

If archaeological flights tend to be made mainly at times when features are visible on the easier soils then the clays will remain largely barren. Flight logs show that this was the case when J.K. St Joseph was virtually the sole archaeological aerial observer in the whole of Britain. He would fly over southern England when crops there were responding to sub-surface features and gradually work his way northwards with the later-ripening crops. As a result, there would have been no one in a position to observe the central England clayland at dates when its crops were responding to buried archaeological features.

Ground survey and excavation

There has recently been an increase in the amount of survey and fieldwork on clay, much of it, in Britain, development (PPG16) related, and some of our contributors are actively involved in this work. This, at last, is beginning to show that this picture of the claylands as barren wasteland is quite often wrong.

At the end of March 2006, a one-day seminar was organised at Cambridge by the archaeological field unit, Albion Archaeology. One aim was to discuss their findings from archaeological excavation undertaken on the route of the A428 road in west Cambridgeshire, but it also allowed time for speakers from the Cambridgeshire County Council Archaeological Field Unit and Cambridge Archaeological Unit to summarise some of their recent work on clays in the region. Those talks were remarkable for the level of detailed information that had been found during excavations and for the general comments that could be made following that work. In Cambridgeshire, there had been occasional visits by people during earlier prehistoric periods but serious occupation of the clayland began during the middle-late Iron Age with ditch-defined farmsteads and field systems. This occupation on clay was seen as a deliberate choice rather than due to people being forced on to 'marginal' land. In fact, Mark Hinman suggested clay was a desirable habitat, not marginal and pointed out that it was drought resistant, produced high yield crops and was also good for pasture. The basic requirement for all settlements is a supply of water and many wells have been discovered on clay. Evidence from molluscs and pollen at some sites show they were located in open grassland during the late Iron Age and an increase in horse bones suggests their breeding was one aspect of many sites' economy. Such an open aspect is contrary to the traditional belief that any occupation on clayland would have been in gloomy clearings within thickly wooded landscapes.

There seemed to be no lessening of occupation density during the Roman period and there was some reuse of older sites and some new foundations. At Longstanton, north-west of Cambridge, work by the Cambridge Archaeological Unit in advance of a new village development enabled Christopher Evans to state that there were population numbers on the clays there that were not reached again until late medieval times. Further west at Love's Farm, St Neots (4), Mark Hinman proposed that hedged boundaries that were established during the late Iron Age and Roman times are still in use and that large tracts of the landscape there follow the same axes that were laid out 2000 years earlier.

A number of small medieval buildings were found in the course of excavations on clay, but it was the village development and open fields that changed the character of the landscape. Extensive areas of medieval ridge and furrow, much of which remained in upstanding form in pasture until the 1960s, covered the landscape and has remained in places to cover earlier features. Ridge and furrow cultivation was responsible for the first plough damage on some prehistoric sites and was noted in some evaluations at the new settlement of Cambourne. It has been suggested that the relatively late conversion of much of the ridge and furrow to modern cultivated land has led to a 'masking' effect in many parts of midland England (Palmer 1996). This, along with the lack of aerial observation, would be another factor that has kept the claylands 'unoccupied' until recent years.

4 Excavations at Love's Farm, St Neots, by Cambridgeshire County Council Archaeological Field Unit in advance of development. The photograph shows part of the stripped 60ha area that was occupied from the late Iron Age to the end of the Roman period, during which time these enclosures were used for habitation, crop processing and animal husbandry. Analysis of molluscs shows the site had been in open grassland that was grazed by cattle, sheep and horses. © *Rog Palmer: 20050803-130, 3 August 2005*

It is important to note how fundamental developer-led (PPG16) work has been in helping us to understand the archaeology of clay landscapes. Unfortunately, minimal academic research has been undertaken on the nature of clayland settlement, as more profitable areas of the landscape such as river gravels and chalk downlands are usually favoured.

CONTRIBUTORS AND STRUCTURE

The book has been divided into three sections: methods, survey and results. Within the methods section, contributions begin with Evans who discusses the importance of rainfall in the development of crop marks. As clay soils and geologies are very water-retentive, dry conditions need to be prolonged throughout the growing season for crop marks to develop on the claylands. As much of Britain and Europe is temperate, this means that conditions for the development of crop marks on clay occur only very occasionally. The problem of commissioning vertical aerial survey to take advantage of such climatic conditions is highlighted by the next contribution by Coleman. Local Governments commission vertical aerial surveys for many different purposes. The difficulty lies in making sure that such surveys are taken at times of the year that suit the recording of archaeological features and this can prove to be difficult with the competing interests of different users. Finally, Grady continues this thread by revealing that national heritage bodies are subject to many contesting demands during an aerial survey. Taking photographs of archaeological crop marks forms only one of many reasons why national bodies take to the air. With pressures on time and resources, finding the right balance between recording productive and unproductive areas of the landscape can be extremely challenging.

The survey section details a number of recent investigations on 'difficult' soils and how current survey methods often struggle to determine archaeological information. Cowley and Dickson's contribution emphasises the role that bias may play in how aerial survey is undertaken. Using eastern and southern Scotland as an example, they examine how blank areas of the landscape (such as clay environs) may indicate biased survey methodologies or the existence of areas that are genuinely devoid of archaeology. This leads on to the paper by Kiarszys, Rączkowski and Żuk which discusses how pre-conceptions and personal agendas may affect the direction of aerial and ground-based surveys. Through comparing the results from aerial survey and Poland's national fieldwalking programme, the authors show how environmental determinism has been a significant factor in how surveys have been directed and undertaken on clay-like soils. This is developed further by Palmer who has examined how observer-directed aerial surveys can mislead through the geographically biased way they are taken. Through comparing the results of the 1996 vertical aerial survey of Bedfordshire with observer-directed photographs, Palmer shows how, under the right conditions, vertical aerial survey has the capacity to record a large number of archaeological sites on the claylands – a feat which traditional aerial photography labours to do. Finally, Oltean and Hanson outline the challenges in determining settlement patterns on 'difficult' soils in Romania. As is typical throughout Britain and Europe, archaeological crop marks are not prolific on clay soils and geologies, and crop marks that do show tend to be of past walled structures and not ditched features.

The results section outlines investigations carried out on the claylands of midland Britain. Significantly, the three contributions show similarities in the form, distribution and chronology of clayland settlement and land use in this particular region. Deegan's examination of the county of Northamptonshire as part of English Heritage's National Mapping Programme, has determined extensive use of clay soils and geologies in prehistory. Site numbers still do not approach those on the more productive geologies such as sands and gravels, nevertheless, aerial photographic evidence points to an upsurge of activity on the clay from the Iron Age onwards. The excavation of an Iron Age banjo enclosure and Romano-British farmstead is the focus of Kenney's paper. Situated on the expanse of clay to the west of Cambridge, the excavation has provided invaluable evidence for the settlement and economy of this long-lived clayland site. The paper by Mills interprets the results of fieldwalking and aerial photographic data for two study areas in north Bedfordshire. Her paper outlines the extensive nature of clayland settlement in this area and how solely using aerial survey as a means for identifying such activity leads to an under-representation of the extent to which clay soils were used. Significantly, evidence points to a clay landscape permeated with Iron Age and Romano-British enclosures centring on animal husbandry.

Finally, Patrick Clay provides a timely summary and prospect of the state of clayland archaeology at the beginning of the twenty-first century. From working for many years on the claylands of midland Britain to completing a doctoral thesis on this subject, Patrick has a valuable insight into the nature of clayland archaeology. Notably, he emphasises the need for more research-led investigations on clay soils and geologies to gain a better understanding of this much neglected area.

CONCLUSION

It is hoped that through compiling this latest clayland research into one volume, a greater awareness of the settlement and use of clay geologies and soils may be elicited. This book may be seen as a 'call to arms' – more research-led investigations on difficult soils and geologies are urgently needed to better determine the extent, form and chronology of archaeological sites on the clay. The fact that many of these clayland sites in Britain and Europe are being gradually ploughed away is a significant factor we all need to bear in mind.

BIBLIOGRAPHY

Abrams, J. & Ingham, D. Forthcoming. Iron Age and Roman settlement remains on the A428 Caxton Common To Hardwick Improvement Scheme, Cambridgeshire.

Allen, G.W.G. 1938. Marks seen from the air in crops near Dorchester. *Oxoniensia* 3, 169-71.

Allen, G.W.G. 1940. Cropmarks seen from the air, Northfield Farm, Long Wittenham, Berks. *Oxoniensia* 5, 164-65.

Benson, D. & Miles, D. 1974. *The Upper Thames Valley: an archaeological survey of the river gravels*. Oxford: Oxford Archaeological Unit.

Bradford, J. 1957. *Ancient landscapes: studies in field archaeology*. London: Bell.

Fulford, M. & Nichols, E (ed.), 1992. *Developing landscapes of Lowland Britain. The archaeology of the British gravels: a review*. Occasional Papers Volume 14: Society of Antiquaries of London.

Mills, J. 2003. Aerial archaeology on clay geologies. *AARGnews* 27, 12-19.

Mills, J. 2005. Bias and the world of the vertical aerial photograph. In K. Brophy & D. Cowley (eds), *From the air: understanding aerial archaeology*, 117-26. Stroud: Tempus.

Palmer, R. 1984. *Danebury: an aerial photographic interpretation of its environs*. RCHM. Supplementary Series 6. London: RCHM.

Palmer, R. 1996. *A further case for the preservation of earthwork ridge and furrow*. Antiquity 70, 436-40.

Palmer, R. 2005. 'If they used their own photographs they wouldn't take them like that'. In K. Brophy & D. Cowley (eds), *From the air: understanding aerial archaeology*, 94-116. Stroud: Tempus.

Phillips, C.W. (ed.), 1970. *The Fenland in Roman times*. London: Royal Geographical Society.

Riley, D.N. 1987. *Air photography and archaeology*. London: Duckworth.

Stoertz, C. 1997. *Ancient landscapes of the Yorkshire Wolds*. Swindon: RCHME.

Webster, G. & Hobley, B. 1965. *Aerial reconnaissance over the Warwickshire Avon*. Archaeological Journal 121, 1-22.

1

The weather and other factors controlling the appearance of crop marks on clay and 'difficult' soils

R. Evans

INTRODUCTION

Air photos taken to record crop marks and patterns are used by two groups of researchers. Archaeologists identify settlements and their surrounding fields from crop marks. Crop patterns help soil scientists explain variations in crop growth within a field and gain a better understanding of soil variability that aids them when mapping and describing soils. Crops grow and yield better over deeper soils. They are taller, greener and denser in the growing season and it is this better growth that is recorded on air photos as darker tones of grey on panchromatic photos or on colour images as greens or yellows and browns when the crop is ripening.

Crop marks can be attributed to the actions of people when they indicate archaeological features such as defensive ditches, ditches separating fields or around buildings or as part of house foundations. Crop patterns are due to natural causes, and indicate that soils, though variable in depth, are generally shallow to a parent material of sand, gravel, chalk, limestones or other hard rocks, or to alternating lithologies of softer (clay, shale) and harder (limestone, sandstone, siltstone, mudstone) rocks. Patterns (Evans 1972; 1990) are often related to periglacial processes at work beyond the margins of the ice during former glaciations. For instance, the widening by ice and infilling by transported material (drift) of bedrock joints in hard rock, or the formation of ice wedge polygons in sand and gravel terraces which on melting were replaced by a drift often of windblown origin, or flow (solifluction) features caused by thawed topsoils flowing over still-frozen subsoil. Former channels can be seen cutting across river and glaciofluvial terrraces. Crop marks and patterns have been recorded widely in England and Wales (Evans 1972; 1990).

Many crop marks and patterns appear during dry weather when the growing crop comes under stress (but see below). However, this period of stress can vary from year to year and if marks and patterns are to be recorded as economically as possible, the aircraft should not take to the air until the weather and soil conditions are appropriate for producing marks and patterns. During dry weather the soils have to provide the moisture which not only supplies the plant nutrients in solution but which is also needed for the crop to transpire. The difference between the amount of outgoing water transpired by the crop and the incoming rainfall can be estimated and, if over the growing season transpiration is greater than rainfall, this Potential Soil Moisture Deficit (PSMD) has to be made up by the soil. Crop patterns (Evans 1972) and marks (Jones and Evans 1975; Evans and Jones 1977) are rarely recorded at PSMDs less than 50mm, which is the approximate amount of water held and released by the plough layer or in soils shallower than about 300mm to rock or sand or gravel.

The work described here ties in with other research being carried out presently to assess runoff and soil erosion from farmers' fields and the transport of pollutants from the land. Field monitoring of runoff, erosion and field-drain flow is carried out and is related to the estimated PSMDs which indicate when soils are drying out, or wetting up, and when soils become saturated and thereafter reach field capacity after about three days of drainage.

THE FORMATION OF PATTERNS AND MARKS

Crop marks and patterns appear when differences in growth within a crop in a field become apparent. Differences in growth can be related to three main causes (Evans and Catt 1987):

1. Differences in availability to the plant of soil moisture and this is related to variations in depth of soil within a field. This cause explains most crop patterns and marks, especially those over sand and gravel or hard rock.

2. Differences in soil colour within a field. Pale coloured soils reflect the incoming sun's energy more than do darker soils and so are cooler. Seeds germinate in them more slowly and plants grow and cover the ground more slowly. Patterns and marks on chalk and chalky till and on alluvial fenland soils are often attributable to this cause and are visible all year round, firstly in bare soil and then in the crop.

3. Differences of soil workability within a field. Topsoils of different texture dry out at different rates, clays more slowly than loamier soils. Drier soils are more easily cultivated and drilled to a crop. When dissimilar topsoils are adjacent to each other within a field the farmer may work the land when the loamier soils become dry enough, but the clays will still be too wet. On the clays the seed will be enclosed within a smeared drill slot, and drainage will be often be poor so the adjacent topsoil is waterlogged and seedling germination is delayed. Such patterns are uncommon, and presently this mechanism cannot be attributed as a cause of soil marks.

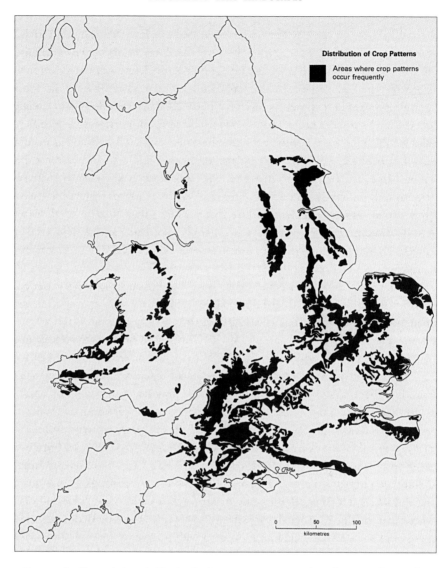

Distribution of Crop Patterns

■ Areas where crop patterns occur frequently

0   50   100

kilometres

5 Extent of soil associations in England where crop patterns and marks occur frequently and extensively

'DIFFICULT' SOILS — APPEARANCE OF CROP MARKS

Aerial archaeologists consider clay soils 'difficult' because crop marks are apparently recorded much less often in clay landscapes than in other landscapes. It is not clear if this lack of crop marks is a result of such landscapes not showing marks or because they were not settled. That clay landscapes were settled is shown by Hall and Hutchings (1972), Simco (1973), Clark and Dawson (1995), Palmer (2005) and Stephen Colman (personal communication) who all record settlements on the chalky till plateau of Bedfordshire and Northamptonshire. Moreover, excavations have revealed sites not only on chalky till

(Luke 2004) but also in the Oxford Clay vale of Bedfordshire (Shotliff and Crick 1999; Dawson 2000). Mills (2003, 2005) shows that crop marks on air photos taken in July 1996 were recorded widely on clay landscapes in Bedfordshire. Even so, in proportion to the extent of soil types, crop marks in Bedfordshire are much more likely to be found on river gravel and alluvium (probably over river gravel) than 'Boulder Clay' (chalky till) or Oxford Clay bedrock. Thus, if crop marks occurred in proportion to the soil's extent the ratio would be 1.00, whereas the ratios between expected and actual occurrence of marks is respectively 1.83 and 1.38 for the valley soils and 0.56 and 0.50 for the clay landscapes. More problematically, in some clay landscapes crop marks or patterns are recorded on soils which lie on a small outcrop of different parent material; for example, river gravel in an instance in Bedfordshire that is more suited to crop mark formation (Clark and Dawson 1995). However, it is not only clay landscapes where crop marks and patterns are rarely recorded. Over much of England and Wales there are many areas where they are rare or not recorded at all (5).

The occurrence of crop patterns and marks was related (Evans 1990) to soil associations portrayed on the Soil Map of England and Wales (SSEW 1983). They occur extensively and frequently in soil associations covering a quarter of England and Wales where land use is dominantly arable and soils are shallow (<80cm, often <60cm) to an impenetrable subsoil. PSMDs in July for winter wheat (SSEW 1984) are on average more than 100mm (*Table 1*). It should be noted that crop patterns do occur extensively on some well-drained clay soils, but these clays are shallow over Jurassic limestone and are not considered as 'clay landscapes' in comparison with the extensive areas (plateaus) of chalky till or the clay vales in East Anglia and Central England. In dry years patterns and marks are recorded extensively in lowland grasslands (*Table 1*). Altogether, patterns and marks occur extensively over almost one-third of England and Wales. Crop patterns and marks are recorded frequently, but not extensively, in soil associations covering about one-quarter of England and Wales which are dominantly in the lowlands and often cultivated (*Table 1*). It is likely that in these associations patterns and marks are recorded where isolated patches of sand and gravel or hard rock outcrop within areas of generally deep soils.

Crop patterns and marks occur rarely or not at all over 37% of England and Wales, where land use is predominantly non arable and PSMDs on average in mid July, for winter wheat, are less than 50mm (*Table 2*). In other words, crop marks and patterns are rare or not recorded where the climate is wetter, land use is not conducive to them showing (grassland, lowland heath, moorland, forests), and soils are deeper and often waterlogged seasonally or for long periods of the year.

In summary, 'difficult' soils for recording crop marks and patterns are those in arable areas which are deep and hold large soil moisture reserves: generally 125mm or more, which is approximately the amount a crop needs to grow and yield well (Smith 1975). This reserve can be released to the crop during spells of dry weather. Outside arable areas where the climate is wetter and grass is the dominant crop, (either as temporary leys or permanent pasture in the lowlands, or as rough grassland alongside the upland moors), is not conducive to showing crop marks. Nor are forests and lowland heaths on poor, often acidic or waterlogged soils. Such soil landscapes cover almost 70% of England and Wales.

Patterns/marks recorded **frequently** and **extensively** in 80 of 296 soil associations

Associations cover 37,664km2, 24.9% of England and Wales

Except one unit, which straddles uplands and lowlands, all units are in the lowlands

Land use is dominantly (74.9%) arable

Only 4.8% of soils are not shallow to hard rock, sand or gravels

PSMDs generally >100mm

Patterns/marks recorded **extensively** in dry years in 14 soil associations

Associations cover 9,884km2, 6.5% England and Wales

All the land is in the lowlands

Land use is dominantly (74%) grassland

Patterns/marks recorded frequently but not extensively in 41 soil associations

Associations cover 35,952km2, 23.8% of England and Wales

Land dominantly (98.5%) in lowlands

Land use is mostly (64.2%) arable

Table 1 Soil associations in which crop patterns and marks occur frequently and extensively

Patterns/marks **rarely** recorded in 61 of 296 soil associations

Associations cover 30,358km², 20.1% of England and Wales

Land dominantly (84.3%) in lowlands

Land use is dominantly (78.6%) not arable

Patterns/marks **not** recorded in 100 soil associations

Associations cover 25,862km², 17.1% of England and Wales

Associations in both lowlands (56%) and uplands (44%)

Land use is predominantly (84.7%) not arable

PSMDs <50mm

Table 2 Soil associations in which crop patterns and marks are rare, or not recorded

16 soil associations cover 16,981km², 11.2% England and Wales
Mostly (64.3%) arable and in lowlands (99%)

Patterns/marks recorded frequently and extensively in one association
   covering 925km², 0.6% England and Wales (5.4% clay lands)

Patterns/marks recorded frequently but not extensively in 7 associations
   covering 12,021km², 7.9% England and Wales (70.8% clay lands)

Patterns/marks rarely recorded in 4 associations covering 2,515km²,
   1.7% England and Wales (14.8% clay lands)

Patterns/marks not recorded in 4 associations covering 1,520km²,
   1.0% England and Wales (8.9% clay lands)

Table 3 Non-alluvial clay soil associations

CLAY LANDSCAPES — APPEARANCE OF CROP MARKS

Clay landscapes, as defined from the National Soil Map (but excluding alluvial clay soil associations), cover only just over one-tenth of England and Wales (SSEW 1983). They occur in the lowlands and are often cultivated (*Table 3*). They account for only a small proportion of the 'difficult' soils where crop marks and patterns are rarely, if at all, recorded. Crop patterns occur widely in one of these associations on Permo-Triassic mudstone and clay shale, but are associated with shallower soils over harder bands of mudstone. Whereas, it is likely that where crop patterns and marks occur frequently but not extensively, they are on patches of drift within the clays as described by Clark and Dawson (1995) in Bedfordshire.

   Crop marks in cultivated clay landscapes were widely recorded on air photos taken of Bedfordshire on 18 July, 1996 (Mills 2003; 2005). The county, or parts of it, has been photographed many times since the mid-1940s, but not often in July (see Coleman; this volume). Much of the land is presently cultivated, and topsoils are often of clay or fine loamy textures on which, because these soils are not always easy to work, a restricted range of crops is grown. These mainly comprise cereals, especially winter wheat, and autumn-sown oilseed rape. The county of Bedfordshire partly abuts Cambridgeshire on its eastern border and soil landscapes are similar on either side of the county boundary, especially where the boundary crosses the chalky till plateau.

   The climate is similar for much of the chalky till plateau of Bedfordshire and Cambridgeshire, although probably being slightly drier and warmer in Cambridgeshire with slightly higher PSMDs (Hodge *et al.* 1984). Monthly rainfall figures are available for the Botanic Garden in Cambridge for a prolonged period (1945-2005), although the

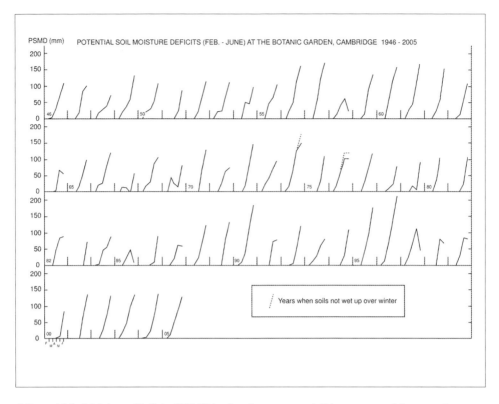

6 Potential Soil Moisture Deficits (PSMDs) of a wheat crop, end-February to end-June, 1946-2005, at Cambridge Botanic Garden

data are published in three differently formatted versions for the years 1945-60, 1961-8 and 1969-91 (Met Office, 1950-63; 1967-74; 1979-93) and latterly, after the Met Office stopped publishing the data, from the office of the Botanic Garden itself. The rainfall data can be used, along with the information in the Ministry of Agriculture, Fisheries and Food Technical Bulletin 16 (Smith 1967) to estimate monthly PSMDs. This was done for the period 1946-2005 — years when air photos were generally available.

PSMDs were calculated by subtracting monthly estimates of evaporation (from the bare soil surface) and transpiration (from the crop) from rainfall and summing the monthly totals. In the period when the crop was growing to cover the ground it was assumed actual evaporation was equal to potential transpiration, which is probably not far from reality (Smith and Douglas 1975). The model used is a simple one; it assumes a green wheat crop transpires at full (potential) rate until mid-July when it stops transpiring as the crop starts to ripen (Feekes growth stage 11.2 (mealy ripe), Thomasson 1979; equivalent to Zadoks growth stage 9 (ripening), FAO, 2005). Barley ripens earlier and oilseed rape flowers in late springtime but continues to grow into the summer period; therefore their PSMDs are likely to be smaller in late June and July than those for wheat.

Other models to estimate PSMD are more elaborate and can incorporate factors which reduce the crop's rate of transpiration when PSMDs reach certain levels assuming

PSMD	Occurrence in 60 years
>50mm	59
>75mm	52
>100mm	35
>125mm	19
>150mm	8
>175mm	3
>200mm	1

Highest max PSMDs: 1995 – 175mm; 1990 – 183mm; 1996 – 211mm

Table 4 Maximum Potential Soil Moisture Deficits reached before or by the end of June at the Botanic Garden, Cambridge, 1946-2005

the crop comes under stress (Smith 1975). The Met Office Rainfall and Evaporation Calculation System (MORECS, Met Office, 2005) is used to calculate soil state and evaporation over large areas (e.g. 40 x 40km). It 'uses a sophisticated equation that calculates soil moisture and evaporation values from measurement of temperature, sunshine, wind and humidity. The equation also allows for local variations in soil type and the crops being grown.' Although the model used here is a simple one it is probably sufficiently accurate for the present purpose. The model has been used in an earlier study to estimate within a day or two when crop patterns appeared at Maxey, Cambridgeshire (Evans and Catt 1987), and is being used presently to estimate, again within a day or two, when soils are saturated and field-drains begin to flow. It is likely that both simple and more complex models give similar results over the growing season until high PSMDs are reached. But above a 100mm deficit, estimates will diverge with values being higher for the simpler model.

Soils wet up in winter (negative PSMD) and were saturated or at field capacity for all winters except those of 1973-4 and 1975-6, when winters were dry and there was no rainfall surplus to the soil's need. The crop's growth would be impeded in the following summer by moisture stress. Soils generally started to dry out (positive PSMD) in February or later and reached a near maximum PSMD by late June. Monthly cumulative PSMDs are plotted (6) from the end of February to the end of June for each year. There is great variation in development of PSMDs from year to year except in the last few years. In only one year did the PSMD not reach 50mm by the end of June (Table 4). And in only one year did the PSMD attain more than 200mm by the end of June – that was in 1996, the year air photos were taken of Bedfordshire.

On average, for the 60-year period 1946 to 2005, the PSMD for the Botanic Garden in Cambridge at the end of June is 108mm. For the end of July, assuming a growing green crop, it is 149mm. It is likely, therefore, that on average by mid-July, when it is assumed the crop has stopped transpiring, PSMD is about 129mm. This is slightly greater than the amount of moisture (115mm) estimated to be held available to the crop by a soil (e.g. Hanslope series) on chalky till at a site about 13km west of Cambridge

(Hodge *et al.* 1984, 211). This assumes cereal roots do not explore beyond a depth of 1.2m of soil (Thomasson 1979). In dry years however, roots may be able to exploit moisture reserves at greater depths. Assuming the subsoil has a dense structure at depth, it is likely that 1.5m of soil will hold somewhere between 150-190mm of water that is available to the crop (after Hodgson 1974, Table 19, 89). Only in very dry years therefore, are crop marks likely to be recorded on clays in Bedfordshire and Cambridgeshire and then only very late on in the growing season.

Air photos have been taken of clay landscapes in west Cambridgeshire from toward the end of June and into late July in 1992 (Palmer, personal communication). Also, from my own experience of examining air photos of the chalky till plateau in northern Bedfordshire, in late June or early July in 1968, 1976 and 1981. It is likely that PSMDs were between 100-135mm respectively in those years. 1976 was a marked drought year where it could have been expected crop marks would have shown on chalky till but they do not appear to have been widespread (Mills and Palmer, personal communication). However, as noted above, the winter of 1975/76 was dry and the soils did not wet up at depth, and it is likely that there was only about 102mm of moisture available to the crop before the roots hit dry soil.

FORMATION OF CROP MARKS IN 'DIFFICULT' SOILS AND CLAY LANDSCAPES

In clay and 'difficult' soil landscapes, excepting marks due to soil colour differences, it is likely to be only in rare years that crop marks are photographed widely. This is because the soils are deep and hold much water that is available to the crop. For crop marks to appear, ditches dug in such soils will have to be deep and contain better structured soils which release more water than the adjacent compact subsoils. There is some evidence for this. In a field in central Norfolk, field boundaries removed in 1962 (Bradley, personal communication) continue to be seen especially later in summer in sugar beet (7) even though on the ground there is no discernible difference in soil colour or other indication of the former ditch. The estimated PSMD at the time the ground photo was taken (18 August 2005) is about 135mm. The soils here are deep over till and of fine loamy texture (clay loam, sandy clay loam) with slowly permeable subsoils and slight seasonal waterlogging. Subsoils in drift parent material, i.e. material that has been displaced from its original position by ice or solifluction, are often denser than those developed in place (*Table 5*) – presumably because the material has become compacted as it has been transported. On average such subsoils are 9% denser and will release about 20% less water to the plant, which over a depth of 0.5m is between 15-20mm of moisture. A similar mechanism could explain the much better growth of grass over field drains seen on closely mown compacted lawns and playing fields in late spring and early summer.

Buried field drains are often recorded as crop marks on air photos. From the little evidence there is, these marks appear to show best in wetter years when PSMDs are low (50-100mm). This suggests that crops above freely draining soils grow better whereas

7 Crop mark developed over a former field ditch infilled in 1962, Bradenham, Norfolk. *Photograph: R. Evans, 18 August 2005*

on the more compact, less freely draining subsoils waterlogging inhibits growth. That this phenomenon may be linked with the compactness of the subsoils is further shown when on some air photos (e.g. Carroll *et al.* 1977, 48-9, plate v) it can be seen that as the field drains pass from chalky till subsoils to subsoils weathered in place in bedrock clay, the drains become less discernible. Mills' (2003; 2005) work suggests that crop marks occur slightly less often on clay soils formed in weathered rock, a ratio of expected occurrence to actual occurrence of 0.50, than in chalky till (ratio 0.56). This again gives some support to the hypothesis that the appearance of crop marks may be related to the degree of compactness of the subsoil.

As noted above, there is much evidence from fieldwalking and archaeological excavations in Bedfordshire and Northamptonshire that the chalky till plateau was settled in prehistoric times. But little of this evidence of settlement appears on air photos. A likely reason for this is that ditches and other archaeological features are often of shallow depth, as Luke's work (2004) at Yarl's Wood shows (*Table 6*). Here, even the deepest feature noted was only 0.4m deep. It is highly unlikely that such shallow features would result in crop marks, unless they were related to differences in soil colour, as there is little difference in exploitable moisture reserves between the archaeological feature and the undisturbed soil.

	Number Horizons	Mean	Median	Range
Subsoils in drift	103	1.496	1.500	1.10-1.80
Subsoils in weathered rock	121	1.370	1.400	0.80-1.80

Information from SSEW (1984) Bulletins 10-15

Table 5 Bulk densities of subsoils (g/cc) developed in drift and weathered rock

Number of archaeological features = 24

Mean depth of feature – 0.20m

Range of depth – 0.05-0.4m

After Luke (2004)

Table 6 Depth of archaeological features at Yarl's Wood, Bedfordshire, on chalky till

CONCLUSIONS

'Difficult' soils for recording crop marks, which includes those in clay landscapes, are deep soils. These soils hold much water available to the plant and archaeological ditches will have to be located deep into the subsoil to exploit any differences in moisture availability.

'Difficult' soils also include those in the wetter parts of Britain where PSMDs rarely exceed 50mm, or which are covered by vegetation less conducive to recording marks such as grassland of various types, lowland heath, and woodland and plantations.

It is likely that in clay landscapes or 'difficult' land under arable land use, to record crop marks, PSMDs as estimated here will need to be higher than 150mm by the end of June. Unless PSMDs are greater than 100mm at the end of May (6) it is unlikely such high PSMDs will be reached by the end of June. Crop marks in cereals on clays therefore, are most likely to be recorded at the very end of the growing season and as the crop starts to ripen.

On clay land and 'difficult' land it is likely that crop marks will show best on soils formed in drift rather than bedrock.

ACKNOWLEDGEMENTS

Staff in the office of Cambridge Botanic Garden were very helpful. Discussions with Anthony Crawshaw, Rog Palmer and John Bradley were also most useful.

BIBLIOGRAPHY

Carroll, D.M., Evans, R. & Bendelow,V.C. 1977. *Air photo-interpretation for soil mapping.* Technical Monograph No. 8, Soil Survey of England and Wales.

Clark, R. & Dawson, M. 1995. Later prehistoric and Romano-British landscape in mid-Bedfordshire. In R. Holgate (ed.), *Chiltern archaeology: recent work: a handbook for the next decade,* 56-68. Dunstable: The Book Castle.

Dawson, M. (ed.) 2000. *Prehistoric, Roman and post-Roman landscapes of the Great Ouse Valley.* York: Council for British Archaeology Research Report 119.

Evans, R. 1972. Air photographs for soil survey in lowland England: soil patterns. *Photogrammetric Record* 7, 302-22.

Evans, R. 1990. Crop patterns recorded on aerial photographs of England and Wales: their type, extent and agricultural implications. *Journal of Agricultural Science* 115, 369-82.

Evans, R. & Catt, J.A. 1987. Causes of crop patterns in eastern England. *Journal of Soil Science* 38, 309-24.

Evans, R. & Jones, R.J.A. 1977. Crop marks and soils at two archaeological sites in Britain. *Journal of Archaeological Science* 4, 63-76.

FAO, 2005. Describing the growth of your crop as stages, www.fao.org/DOCREP/006/x8234E/x8234e05.html (accessed 12 December 2005)

Hall, D.N. & Hutchings, J.B. 1972. Distribution of archaeological sites between the Nene and Ouse valleys. *Bedfordshire Archaeological Journal* 1, 1-16.

Hodge, C.A.H., Burton, R.G.O.B., Corbett,W.M., Evans, R. & Seale, R.S. 1984. *Soils and their use in Eastern England.* Bulletin 15, Soil Survey of England and Wales.

Hodgson, J.M. (ed.) 1974. *Soil Survey field handbook.* Technical Monograph No. 5, Soil Survey of England and Wales.

Jones, R.J.A. & Evans, R. 1975. Soil and crop marks in the recognition of archaeological sites by air photography. In D.R. Wilson (ed.), *Aerial reconnaissance for archaeology,* 1-11. York: Council for British Archaeology Research Report 12.

Luke, M. 2004. Evidence for prehistoric settlement and medieval activity at Yarl's Wood, Clapham. *Bedfordshire Archaeology* 25, 3-22.

Met. Office 1950-1963. *British rainfall (1945-1960).* London: HMSO.

Met. Office 1967-1974. *British rainfall (1961-1968).* London: HMSO.

Met. Office 1979-1993. *Monthly and annual totals of rainfall (1969-1991).* London: HMSO.

Met. Office 2005. MORECS, www.metoffice.gov.uk/environment/morecs.html (accessed 12 December 2005).

Mills, J. 2003. Aerial archaeology on clay geologies. *AARGnews* 27, 12-19.

Mills, J. 2005. Bias and the world of the aerial photograph. In K. Brophy & D. Cowley (eds), *From the air: understanding aerial archaeology,* 117-26. Stroud: Tempus.

Palmer, R. 2005. And the cover photo? *AARGnews* 31, 4.

Shotliff, D. & Crick, J. 1999. Iron Age settlement within the Oxford Clay Vale at Beancroft Road, Marston Moretaine. *Bedfordshire Archaeology* 23, 32-42.

Simco, A. 1973. The Iron Age in the Bedford region. *Bedfordshire Archaeology* 8, 5-22.

Smith, L.P. 1967. *Potential transpiration.* Technical Bulletin No. 16, Ministry of Agriculture, Fisheries and Food. London: HMSO.

Smith, L.P. 1975. *Methods in agricultural meteorology.* Oxford: Elsevier.

Smith, L.P. & Douglas, H.A. 1975. Theoretical considerations of the water loss by evaporation from bare soil and the effect of partial crop cover. *ADAS Quarterly Review* 16, 135-44.

SSEW, 1983. *Legend for the 1:250,000 soil map of England and Wales.* Soil Survey of England and Wales.

SSEW, 1984. *Soils and their use in (Northern England; Wales; Midland and Western England; Eastern England; South West England; South East England),* Bulletins 10-15, Soil Survey of England and Wales.

Thomasson, A.J. 1979. Assessment of soil droughtiness. In M.G. Jarvis & D. Mackney (eds), *Soil survey applications,* 43-50. Technical Monograph 13, Soil Survey of England and Wales.

2

Taking advantage:
vertical aerial photographs
commissioned for local authorities

Stephen Coleman

INTRODUCTION

The main inspiration both for this volume and the conference preceding it was the archaeological results obtained on clay soils from a vertical aerial survey of Bedfordshire commissioned in 1996 by my employers, Bedfordshire County Council.

However, 1996 was not the first such flight over Bedfordshire as the County Council has commissioned whole county vertical aerial photography several times since 1968 for general rather than archaeological purposes. Vertical photographs are taken automatically looking straight down in plan view from an aircraft flying north–south or east–west parallel traverses at a uniformly level height to achieve a near consistent scale. In Bedfordshire this has usually meant flying at 5000ft (1524m) to produce imagery at a scale of 1:10,000. The photos are taken to the Royal Institute of Chartered Surveyors specification of 60% forward overlap and 25 or 30% lateral overlap. This allows for stereoscopic viewing and hence topographic or three dimensional analysis – which is one of the key benefits of vertical photography. An additional advantage is that features identified on vertical photographs can be mapped without the need for specialist techniques or software.

AERIAL PHOTOGRAPHS AT BEDFORDSHIRE COUNTY COUNCIL

Other counties have commissioned similar flights over the years, but generally, this occurs less frequently. This is probably due to the fact that Bedfordshire is one of the smallest counties, at 1192sq km, and is therefore less costly to fly on a regular basis. Even so, Bedfordshire has only been flown every five years or so, in 1968, 1976, 1981, 1986, 1991, 1996 and 2002. The first four years were taken in black and white and the last three in colour, 2002 also being obtained digitally. Each of these flights has produced around 1,000 nine by nine inch square prints which in itself is a challenge from the point of view of storage. In addition, we possess excellent black and white vertical coverage of the county taken by the RAF immediately after the Second World War, mainly in 1946 and 1947, totalling over 3,000 prints. These have been particularly useful for mapping earthwork landscapes, including much now-destroyed ridge and furrow.

Although my role has long included responsibility for the RAF aerial photographs and our collection of over 2200 observer-directed oblique aerial photographs of archaeological sites, it is only since one of our County Council reorganisations in 1997 that I have had care of all the other aerial photographs and, indeed, was responsible for commissioning our 2002 flight. Not that I, or my archaeological colleagues and predecessors, lacked interest in these verticals before. Indeed, we and they were consulting them from the early days of archaeological services being provided by the County Council from the mid 1970s and were also contributing to the commissioning process from that time. In fact, the first flight benefiting from archaeological advice was that in 1976. This was one of the driest years on record and it was possible for the photography to be carried out at around the optimum time in late June/early July. Numerous previously unknown crop marks were recorded in various parts of the county, especially on the gravels but, strikingly, not usually on the clays. The flight in 1981 was also carried out at the likely optimum time, from mid-June to early July, but in fact the photographs were of little value archaeologically on any of the county's soils. Also those taken previously in 1968, 50% of them in June and July, were only marginally more useful. Clearly climatic and soil conditions in the months prior to these two flights in 1968 and 1981 were not suitable for crop marks to develop, unlike the same time in 1976. From an archaeological point of view the next two flights in 1986 and 1991 suffered from the commercial flying company's desire to wait and wait and wait for the whole of the county to be totally cloud free for all of one or two days in order to limit flying time or avoid having to repeat part of the flight. This resulted in photographs being taken in August and September, after harvest and just before the end of the flying season and thus of little archaeological value.

AERIAL PHOTOGRAPHS IN 1996

And then came 1996, another dry year, with the photography largely undertaken on one day, 18 July, though some was also carried out on the three days before. The results were spectacular: not only were numerous previously known crop marks visible, often with additional features apparent, but nearly 400 previously unidentified discrete areas of crop marks, from extensive complexes down to single enclosures, were recorded in Bedfordshire alone. In addition, crop mark evidence was now added to 35 (or nearly one third) of the 113 Roman and pre-Roman sites and slag patches identified by David Hall and colleagues during fieldwalking between the early 1960s and early 1970s in 12 mainly clay parishes in north-west Bedfordshire (see Mills; this volume). Over large parts of north Bedfordshire (and beyond into Northamptonshire and Cambridgeshire), tracts of previously apparently empty countryside on the calcareous Boulder Clay were now filled by crop mark evidence. Clearly David Hall's and John Hutching's statement that 'aerial photography detects few clayland sites', which appears at the beginning of their 1972 paper detailing fieldwalking results, had to be revised (Hall and Hutchings 1972, 1). Nevertheless, a substantial number of their sites on clay still have no known associated crop marks. I should also add that in 1996 previously unknown crop marks were not just identified on the north Bedfordshire Boulder Clays, but there were also a few on the Oxford Clay in the Marston Vale and others in the Gault clay vale sandwiched between the chalk and greensand towards the south of the county. Sites were also identified on the greensand ridge, but many of these probably occupy non-sandy soil deposits over the greensand.

However, the significance of the 1996 flight for me is not just the archaeological features themselves, but the broader landscape context which vertical photographs allow them to be seen in: the height from which the photographs are taken enables good sized areas to be viewed. Archaeological relationships can be seen (or not) and relationships with geology and topography. Most importantly, though, whole relict fluvial landscapes are revealed by the 1996 photographs – hundreds of now dry minor stream courses. The vast majority of newly identified crop marks of sites on the north Bedfordshire clays lie on high ground, particularly along ridge tops, now, seemingly, with no water supply nearby. However, the 1996 photographs show most were originally placed near, or were closely associated with, the headwaters of minor streams or with springs (even sometimes enclosing the latter) in prehistoric or Roman times. We can thus see sites set in their 'natural' environment.

I am emphasising the archaeological value of the 1996 aerial photographs, but it should not be forgotten that there had already been an inkling that the north Bedfordshire clays were not a lost cause for crop marks. In June and July 1984 a good number of archaeological crop marks were newly identified through the oblique photography of Ken Field and, in particular, Glenn Foard. They also found a few more in 1986, again in June and July. But why have crop marks seemingly only become apparent here since the mid 1980s? Also, despite these recent discoveries not all existing sites have been identified by aerial photographs: recent archaeological work on constructing the Great Barford Bypass north-east of Bedford revealed previously unknown sites in an area apparently well documented by aerial photographs.

PROBLEMS FOR LOCAL AUTHORITIES

I have highlighted some of the advantages of vertical photography taken countywide, but what of the disadvantages? For a local authority, and presumably most large organisations bound by annual budgets, many of the disadvantages stem from the fact that the planning and commissioning of a flight has to be carried out well ahead of it actually taking place due to budgetary procedures and the tendering process. Our vertical flights cannot be reactive which can be the key advantage of oblique photography: you can get up and go when sites are known to be visible, though I find it strange that nobody seems to have taken obliques of our 1996 sites! It was pure luck that a vertical flight was planned for 1996. But should it be left to luck? Is it possible to arrange reactive vertical flying at short notice?

A key problem for local authorities is that because the flights are not commissioned every year there is usually no annually recurring budget. A case for funding has to be made each time and that funding has to be confirmed before the end of the financial year, i.e. March, or sometimes earlier, preceding the chosen summer flying season. Then the tendering process has to be gone through, quotes usually being obtained from 3 companies. All in all it is a rigid, time-consuming, process. In most cases, planning for the Bedfordshire vertical flights seems to have begun about a year before the flight was actually required, although much of that planning related to raising the finance. For several years the County Planning Department, which included my area of work, had responsibility for the aerial photographs, being managed and held through its Drawing Office (now long gone). That Office's principal officer commissioned the flights between 1968 and 1996, discussing the proposals with interested parties such as ourselves and pursued funding. Some of the correspondence requesting financial support from other Departments and their subsequent responses are quite entertaining but, essentially, although many were interested in using the photographs, such as Highways, Rights of Way, and Education, none of them were willing to put money into the pot. Despite being a corporate resource, the flights were mostly funded by the County Planning Department in partnership with the District Councils.

COSTS

Here I should provide some idea of the costs involved. In 1981 the flight, one set of black and white nine by nine inch square contact prints and an index plot cost just under £12,000 excluding VAT, with Bedfordshire County Council retaining the copyright. In 1986, to reduce the cost, the County Council relinquished copyright of that year's flight to the commissioned company and paid £9950 excluding VAT. In 1991, the first colour survey, copyright was again relinquished giving a cost of £14,800 (it would have been £8900 for black & white). Unfortunately I have no record of costs for 1996.

COMMISSIONING AERIAL PHOTOGRAPHS

Our most recent flight was in 2002, with which I was directly involved. Following the very major restructuring of the Council's organisational setup in 1997, the old Departments disappeared to be replaced by numerous smaller units. Little or no thought was given to how future provision of corporately used resources, such as aerial photographs, would be arranged and funded. Responsibility for care and management of the existing collections had been added to my job, but then with another flight due in 2001 the commissioning role also fell to me, beginning in August 2000. A meeting in September was arranged to which all the likely interested County Council and District Council parties were invited. Many did not come – perhaps most surprisingly nobody from Highways and Transport attended. However, the strategic planners, Rights of Way officers and Minerals and Waste team were keen whilst there was also representation from Education, Emergency Planning, Libraries and the County Record Office.

For the first time, obtaining seamless digital photography was discussed and was strongly supported by the planners and Rights of Way officers. Discussions also included when exactly the flight should be carried out: although several parties had no preferred time, the consensus of the others was June/July fitting in with archaeological preferences. I then prepared a business case to pursue funding which is when the real problems began. Although I had support from the District Councils, raising a budget within the County Council was difficult due to the changes of 1997 and the lack of corporateness. To cut a long story short, it was only the prospect of obtaining digital data for inclusion in the corporate Geographical Information System (GIS) which won the day and the money was finally approved in August 2001, sadly a year after the process had begun and after the flight should have taken place.

Despite a rapid tendering process, climatic conditions and flying restrictions imposed as a result of the 9/11 attacks in New York, meant that the flight could not be carried out before the end of the 2001 flying season in October. This further emphasises the difficulties of arranging vertical photography over a sizeable area. The flight was eventually carried out early in the following year's flying season over the Jubilee weekend 31 May to 2 June 2002. The resulting images were dominated by lush green vegetation and were of little archaeological value in either print or digital format, though the County Council's arboriculturalists have found it particularly useful for the study of individual trees and woodland within a GIS environment. For the record, the cost for a flight of 806km in length producing 994 contact prints and an index plot with copyright relinquished was £13,500, i.e. lower than previous surveys, possibly due to the influence of the various Millennium photography projects. Even so, costs do seem to have been coming down. Obtaining the digital data added another £3500. As copyright was relinquished to the company commissioned to supply the photography, they can license it elsewhere and currently it is the source of the Bedfordshire coverage on Google Earth. The latter, which is freely accessible, and the dissemination of the results of the various Millennium projects have raised the profile of aerial photography, not only with the public but also within local authorities, particularly the District Councils. There is now greater interest in obtaining such material but in digital format only for incorporation into GIS rather than as prints.

THE FUTURE

In future we will probably only be able to source funding for digital vertical photography. In recent months, several companies have started to offer aerial images licensed for three years to include all updates of tiles during the term, i.e. complete county coverage will not necessarily be all of the same date! They also guarantee reflights every three years. A District Council led consortium for Bedfordshire has just placed an order for such photography but this means that we, as archaeologists, and the County Council have lost our influence on how and when the photography is done.

My title (suggested some time ago) starts with the words Taking Advantage: but in fact we may have lost our chance! Nevertheless, some way needs to be found to tap into the benefits which vertical photography provides for archaeology, particularly if we can find some way of utilising it at relatively short notice. This may be possible as the monitoring of soil moisture deficits could provide a reactive lead-in time of two months (see R. Evans; this volume).

BIBLIOGRAPHY

Hall, D.N. & Hutchings, J.B. 1972. The Distribution of Archaeological Sites between the Nene and the Ouse Valleys. *Bedfordshire Archaeological Journal* 7, 1-16.

3

Crop marks on clay – getting the timing right

Damian M. Grady

INTRODUCTION

The organisers of the conference at Leicester asked me to talk about the reconnaissance techniques that English Heritage (EH) applies to finding 'crop-marked archaeological features' on clay soils. Archaeological and geological features beneath the plough soil can visibly affect the growth of crops over them (R. Evans; this volume), and for more than 80 years archaeologists have seen the value of the aerial perspective for the identification of archaeological sites visible as crop marks. My approach to crop mark reconnaissance over clay and other difficult soils has changed little since my thoughts on the subject were expressed at the Aerial Archaeology Research Group conference in Bournemouth in 1999 (Grady 2000). My views at Bournemouth were influenced by the quantity of new sites discovered on difficult soils in the drought year of 1996. Unfortunately, since starting my flying duties in 1998, the weather conditions have not been conducive to the production of large numbers of crop marks on any geology, not just the difficult ones. This immediately poses a problem for anyone planning or executing an aerial survey with the prime aim of recording crop marks.

This chapter will outline the way in which the EH reconnaissance teams in Swindon and York make use of the observer-led flying technique to assess crop mark potential on all geologies, whilst having the flexibility to undertake other survey work when crop marks do not appear. Areas where sites have been found on difficult soils in generally poor years for crop marks will then be discussed.

ENGLISH HERITAGE OBSERVER–LED RECONNAISSANCE

The EH reconnaissance teams take to the air with previous experience of archaeological excavation, air photo interpretation and mapping along with a general knowledge of the landscape archaeology of all periods from the Neolithic to the present day. High-winged Cessna 172s based at Oxford and Sherburn-in-Elmet are available at short notice as is a small team of pilots; 1:50,000 maps are used to navigate. The maps are marked with mapped archaeology, scheduled monuments, sites from the Parks and Gardens register and specific targets requested by a variety of specialists. Such annotated maps allow more time to be spent looking for new sites rather than re-photographing known ones. Once a decision is made about recording a site, the archaeologist directs the pilot to position the aircraft appropriately. If a site is to be mapped, photographs must be taken as near to vertical as possible with control points, and sometimes detailed shots of complex elements of the site are taken to aid interpretation.

Throughout the year the Meteorological Office Soil Moisture Deficit (SMD) data are assessed to anticipate the development of crop marks. When figures reach 50, crop marks should start to appear and when they reach 100 they should be very distinctive (Jones and Evans 1975), especially on well-drained soils (R. Evans; this volume). When the SMD figures reach 150 then, with luck, crop marks on clay should begin to appear. The SMD figures can only be a guide to which areas of the country are most likely to have stressed crops. Other variables such as the crop type and the point in the growing cycle also need to be taken into consideration. In the end, the best way to make an assessment of crop mark potential is to get airborne. During a summer flying season, assessment of crop conditions is made by looking for signs of drainage, geological or archaeological features that are affecting crop growth. In an average year one would normally expect to see some known sites: this gives an indication as to whether it is worth undertaking a more systematic reconnaissance. Some aerial archaeologists would argue that if these indicator sites are not visible, one should return to the airfield. This approach is not entirely satisfactory. Sampling areas by undertaking a few systematic transects is preferable. Even if crops on the so called 'honey-pot' geologies (chalk, gravel, fens, etc.) reveal crop marks it is important to assess clay areas when transiting between productive zones or to target sites known on clay from fieldwalking, etc. to assess the area for crop mark potential.

Another important source of information on crop conditions is other flyers. Throughout the spring and summer the majority of those actively involved in aerial reconnaissance in all parts of Britain report, via e-mail, on their success or otherwise in finding crop marks. This information is circulated to those interested or involved in helping to plan further flights.

Crop marks in wheat appear a week or two later on clay compared to other geologies, so in the south of England they appear in late July and early August and have a tendency to reveal themselves just as the harvest is underway. They are usually poorly defined and difficult to see from certain angles. The directional nature of the crop marks means that, when possible, the survey has to be undertaken in a systematic way. Each field is assessed from more than one angle, assuming that wind and cloud cover will allow it. The 1996 crop mark season was exceptional partly because it was the culmination of a number of dry years, but also as a result of a dry spring and early summer. Since 1996 there has been either a wet spring or wet summer or both. Occasionally there have been spells of very dry weather in late summer. The latter have been too late to affect wheat growth over archaeological features before harvest, but have helped bring on crop marks in sugar beet, even in some clay areas such as Suffolk. However, the days of finding crop marks in late August and September in sugar beet are likely to end soon with the reduction in agricultural subsidies for this crop.

Whilst some archaeologists equate aerial photography with crop marks, aerial reconnaissance is also used to record other forms of landscape feature to assist other heritage professionals. On any one flight photographs could be taken of crop marks, earthworks, scheduled monuments, parks and gardens and buildings. Each type of site requires a different style of photography; crop marks require control points and stereo pairs for mapping, as do earthworks. Photography of scheduled monuments for monitoring purposes may need general shots to assess land use in adjacent fields or detailed shots to record damage caused by animal burrowing or encroachment by invasive vegetation such as bracken. Buildings can range from closely spaced workshops in an urban setting, to large complexes such as Cold War sites or landscape parks and gardens. In practice, two or three of these types of sites dominate a flight in a year when crop marks are average, but in a drought year recording of crop marks is likely to dominate the summer flying programme. When there is no drought, clay areas still need to be assessed, but in undertaking any form of aerial survey in the hope of finding crop marks there is always the potential for disappointment. An observer-led flight that includes a target list of sites other than just crop marks in this situation allows flexibility and ensures a flight is not wasted if crop marks are limited. There is always a danger that by attempting to balance the needs of a variety of users, crop mark reconnaissance flights are pushed down the priority list. In reality the reverse is true, especially in an exceptionally dry year, as other landscape features and buildings can be photographed at other times of the year.

OBLIQUES OR VERTICALS?

The 1996 vertical survey of Bedfordshire not only revealed a vast number of new sites on the clay, but led to calls for the replacement of oblique photographs produced by observer-led reconnaissance with vertical survey (Palmer 2005 and this volume). David Wilson (2005) has recently suggested that to argue for one technique over the other is erroneous – verticals and obliques each have their place. The problems of setting up and executing a vertical survey are highlighted by Stephen Coleman (this volume). As vertical survey has to be commissioned well in advance, there is the danger that when it comes to the day of survey, conditions are far from ideal. However, when flown at the right time, as in 1996, the results can be stunning. The strength of the observer-led approach is that flights can usually be arranged at very short notice and as such this technique is more flexible when conditions are rapidly changing. Under certain circumstances aspects of vertical photography can be mimicked in a Cessna 172, such as stereo pairs and block flying. Vertical surveys have been commissioned at short notice by EH to cover relatively small areas, such as Fylingdales (Horne *et al.* 2005). However, we still need to be able to commission vertical surveys over larger areas at short notice when conditions similar to those in 1996 re-occur.

ATTITUDES TO CLAY AND OTHER 'DIFFICULT' SOILS

Some have been critical of aerial archaeologists' lack of interest in clay landscapes. Chris Taylor in 1975 pointed out that the distribution of aerial photographs on mainly light soils had distorted our understanding of past land use. Initially Taylor targeted his criticism on the pre-war flyers, but suggested that this attitude was still prevalent in the mid-1970s. Given the ease with which sites could be found on light soils, the damage caused to archaeological remains by gravel extraction (RCHME 1960) and the conversion of pasture to arable (Riley 1983), it is no surprise that this bias occurred. But as Brophy (2005) asks, is there anything wrong with bias and subjectivity as long as we recognise it, understand it and develop strategies to overcome it?

We know that some of our predecessors told us that we would not see archaeological crop marks on clay. This attitude may have come from their own experience or have been picked up from other flyers. This has resulted in a vicious circle; you do not find crop marks on clay, therefore you do not fly over clay and so no new sites are found on clay. Without flight traces from Global Positioning Systems it is not always easy to recreate the routes taken by many flyers before the 1990s; therefore we have to rely on their flight reports and the photographs taken (Oakey 2005). Undoubtedly some will have flown over clay areas and kept looking for crop marks on their way to the 'honey-pot' areas. Without knowing earlier flyers personally, it is difficult to defend or attack their attitude to clay soils, but we must also bear in mind that clay landscapes in the 1950s, '60s and '70s may have been different to those we see today. In some areas the balance of pasture to arable will have been different and there would have been more upstanding medieval ridge and furrow. The gradual levelling of medieval ridge and furrow by post-war ploughing is destroying this protective layer (Palmer 1996) making the earlier archaeological features more vulnerable to destruction, but also more visible from the air as crop marks (*8*). Of course this is an over-simplification, but an understanding of where ridge and furrow has been lost will help target areas for new discoveries (Bishop *et al.* 2005).

Following project work in the Vale of York (Swan *et al.* 1993) in an area with difficult soils and learning about the 1996 Bedfordshire survey, the view I expressed at Bournemouth was that aerial archaeologists need to target clay soils more often to address the apparent bias in the distribution of aerial photographs. The response to my paper varied, from those who still believed that difficult soils were unproductive to those who insisted they should be a priority. Others were worried that difficult soils were being considered more important than other areas. However, there did seem to be a consensus that difficult soils should be targeted in exceptional drought years.

8 Crop marks of prehistoric features visible through ploughed-out ridge and furrow on Kimmeridge clay in the Vale of the White Horse, Oxfordshire. Part enlargement of *NMR 21244/04 21-JUN-2001 © English Heritage*

Today the minds of all the active flyers are open to the potential of finding crop marks on difficult soils. When I took over flying responsibilities from Roger Featherstone in 1998, I highlighted the problems of the aerial photographic coverage in clay-dominated counties like Suffolk. In other areas people like Davy Strachan and Helen Saunders have covered the clay soils in Essex, Ben Robinson flies over Huntingdonshire, Chris Musson covers Herefordshire, Chris Cox has covered the Bourn area of Cambridgeshire and in the south-west Francis Griffiths and Steve Hartgroves have to contend with difficult soils over most of their area.

However, with the best will in the world, finding crop marks on clay is still a challenge. Whether one is engaged in observer-led flying or commissioning vertical photography, crop marks on clay may be few and far between.

POOR TO AVERAGE YEARS FOR THE DEVELOPMENT OF CROP MARKS ON CLAY

While being open to actively looking for crop marks in difficult areas, recent conditions have not been conducive to finding many sites. In 2000 EH highlighted the need for more reconnaissance in parts of East Anglia, mainly Suffolk, and the West Midlands (Grady 2000). In the research agendas for these areas too there is a belief that 'aerial survey is the only long-term research which is producing valuable new data about the archaeological resource on a regional basis' (Wade and Brown 2000, 55); there is also still a need to understand what has already been photographed (Barber in press). However, in the last five years the West Midlands has seen low SMD figures and reconnaissance for crop marks by EH and other flyers has not been very productive.

Compared to the West Midlands, the east of England has seen drier conditions and flying for recent mapping projects, scheduled monument monitoring, architectural projects and landscape photography has provided the opportunity to monitor clay soils in East Anglia. In Suffolk the distribution of crop marks is still biased towards the lighter soils, despite the best efforts of Robert Carr who flew over the Boulder Clay in the 1980s and early 1990s. Fieldwalking has played an important part in the discovery of new sites of all periods on the Suffolk clay. Warner's analysis of greens, commons and documentary evidence paints a complex picture of late Saxon settlement (Warner 1987). Tom Williamson's (1987) analysis of possible prehistoric field systems visible in the modern field patterns in Norfolk indicates that similar patterns may occur in parts of Suffolk. It would appear that the archaeologists of Suffolk seem to be investigating the clay productively without new aerial photography. Nonetheless, whilst undertaking project work on the light soils of the Sandlings and the tributaries of the Stour Valley, it has been possible to look at the Boulder Clay areas as well. This has led to the discovery of a small number of new sites; mainly ring ditches and rectilinear enclosures, which gives enough hope that more will be found in this area in drier conditions.

In the last five years, roughly the same amount of time has been spent flying over the Suffolk clays as over those in Bedfordshire. In 1998, Rog Palmer provided a distribution map of the sites seen on the 1996 Bedfordshire verticals (reproduced in this volume). Although this was only complete for the area to the east of the river Ivel, it offered an opportunity to target known sites to assess crop mark development in an area dominated by Oxford, Gault and Boulder Clay. Unfortunately, when crop marks appeared on the river gravels the clay was disappointing and even a few weeks later only a handful of the sites photographed in 1996 were visible in the Palmer study area. However, in 2003 and 2005 on the Boulder Clay in north Bedfordshire and north of Milton Keynes, crop marks were visible mainly in fields of ripe wheat. The year 2003 had a hot, dry summer, but the opportunities for flying in late June/early July had been hampered by cloud. In late July/early August the conditions were such that the harvest seemed to have been brought forward by a week or two. Many of the crop marks in both years were not very well defined and at times very fragmentary (9), but it was an encouraging sign that in an average summer there is potential for recording new sites on clay. We have not yet

9 Curvilinear enclosures near Shrubbery Farm in Wilden parish, Bedfordshire. Many of the crop marks visible on this flight were very fragmentary and difficult to record because of overcast conditions. *NMR23173/11 05-AUG-2003 © English Heritage*

analysed all the recent material and suspect that many of the sites will have already been identified on the 1996 survey, but we expect to find that the Boulder Clay was more productive than the Oxford clay (Mills; this volume).

Over the last five years the Bedfordshire clay had been more productive than other clay areas, especially Suffolk. Both Bedfordshire and west Suffolk have large tracts of land covered with the same Hanslope association soil type on Boulder Clay, although the solid geology is different; mainly Oxford clay in North Bedfordshire and chalk in Suffolk. Is the Bedfordshire clay atypical, is the archaeology different, or has it been too badly damaged in Suffolk to be visible as crop marks any more? Further aerial reconnaissance, especially over clay soils formed on drift rather than solid geology (R. Evans; this volume), and refinement of the use of SMD data may provide some answers.

EXMOOR

At this point it is worth mentioning the work EH has been doing in partnership with Exmoor National Park on another area of difficult soils. Over the last ten years EH has been photographing mainly earthwork sites on Exmoor for the Park's archaeologist to use for monitoring, interpretation and educational purposes. However, since 2005 the emphasis has changed a little. The Park's archaeologist, Robert Wilson-North, has written a research strategy, which highlights the need to learn more about archaeology that does not survive as upstanding remains. To this end aerial reconnaissance has begun to target the pasture of the Brendon Hills for parchmarks and the arable area between the Brendon Hills and the coast for crop marks. Despite having difficult soils on sandstone, siltstone, mudstone and slate there is potential for crop mark formation in arable as has been demonstrated by the few sites that have been found in previous years. The pasture areas of the Brendon Hills have yet to show any potential. In the first year, 2005, only two crop marks have been photographed, one was a known site of a typical late prehistoric hill-slope enclosure on relatively thin soil, the other being a fragmentary linear feature. The first year of flying has been disappointing, but it is possible that new discoveries could be made in arable areas. It will be more challenging to find sites in pasture, especially given the rarity of dry soil conditions in the west (R. Evans; this volume).

'HONEY-POT' AREAS

Within the traditional 'honey-pot' areas it must be remembered that the geology is not uniform and there are areas where crop marks have rarely been found. For example, few sites have been identified to the north-west of Avebury where there is a capping of clay with flints. However, this area is within the Military Air Traffic Zone of Lyneham airfield, which has limited access for archaeological reconnaissance. In other chalk areas, such as the North Downs, the soils are not as helpful as one would like. John Hampton flew from nearby Biggin Hill, but photographed few crop marks in the area when compared to the productive chalk to the east of the A2 in Kent.

CONCLUSION

Today the minds of the majority of aerial archaeologists are open to looking for crop marks on difficult soils. One of the main advantages of observer-led reconnaissance with a large portfolio of targets is that it allows for the flexibility to assess areas and move on as necessary, undertaking survey work for those interested in all aspects of the historic landscape. The main problem with difficult soils is that they are difficult; they will only reveal large numbers of crop marks in exceptional conditions especially in the west of the country. Flying in the east in years when crop marks are average has revealed new sites on clay, but not in such quantities as to alter the existing archaeological narrative. Finding new sites on clay is going to take time unless there is another dramatic drought year. In the meantime, we need to map and understand the sites already photographed, make more use of other remote sensing techniques and refine our use of SMD data. The latter will be particularly important for judging when there is going to be another exceptional summer drought, not only assisting observer-led reconnaissance, but also enabling vertical surveys to be commissioned in time for the potential appearance of more crop marks on clay.

BIBLIOGRAPHY

Barber, M. In Press. The blank country? Neolithic enclosures and landscapes in the West Midlands. In P. Garwood (ed.), *The undiscovered country. The earlier prehistory of the West Midlands.* The Making of the West Midlands vol 1. Oxford: Oxbow.

Bishop, S., Small, F., Stoertz, C. & Carpenter, E. 2005. Gloucestershire NMP and ridge and furrow ploughing. In T. Wilmot (ed.), *Research News: newsletter of the English Heritage Research Department* 1, 21.

Brophy, K. 2005. Subjectivity, bias and perception in aerial archaeology. In K. Brophy & D. Cowley (eds), *From the air: understanding aerial archaeology,* 33-49. Stroud: Tempus.

Grady, D.M. 2000. Aerial reconnaissance in England: some thoughts for the future. *AARGnews* 20, 15-26.

Horne, P., Macleod, D. & Stone, J. 2005. Out of the ashes: responding to the Great Fylingdales fire. In T. Wilmot (ed.), *Research News: newsletter of the English Heritage Research Department* 1, 22-24.

Jones, R.J.A. & Evans, R. 1975. Soil and crop marks in the recognition of archaeological sites by air photography. In D. Wilson (ed), *Aerial reconnaissance for archaeology,* 1-11. *Council for British Archaeology Research Report* 12: York.

Oakey, M. 2005. Patterns of aerial photography in the Central Midlands of England: evaluating biases in past programmes of aerial reconnaissance and their potential impact. In K. Brophy & D. Cowley (eds), *From the air: understanding aerial archaeology,* 141-50. Stroud: Tempus.

Palmer, R. 1996. A further case for the preservation of earthwork ridge-and-furrow. *Antiquity* 70: 268, 436-40.

Palmer, R. 2005. If they used their own photographs they would not take them like that. In K. Brophy & D. Cowley (eds), *From the air: understanding aerial archaeology,* 94-116. Stroud: Tempus.

RCHME. 1960. *A matter of time: an archaeological survey.* London: HMSO.

Riley, D. 1983. The frequency of occurrence of cropmarks in relation to soils. In G.S. Maxwell (ed.), *The impact of aerial reconnaissance on archaeology,* 59-73. CBA Research Report 49: York.

Swan, V.G., Jones, B.E.A. & Grady, D. 1993. Bolesford, North Riding of Yorkshire: lost wapentake and its landscape. *Landscape History* 15: 13-28.

Taylor, C.C. 1975. Aerial photography and the field archaeologist. In D.R. Wilson (ed.), *Aerial reconnaissance for archaeology,* 136-41. *CBA Research Report* 12: York.

Wade, K. & Brown, N. 2000. Research strategy. In N. Brown & J. Glazebrook (eds), *Research and archaeology: a framework for the Eastern Counties,* 50-8. East Anglian Archaeology Occasional Papers 8.

Warner, P. 1987. *Greens, commons and clayland colonization: the origins and development of green-side settlement in East Suffolk.* Department of English Local History Occasional Papers fourth series, 2. Leicester: Leicester University Press.

Williamson, T. 1987. Early co-axial field systems in East Anglia. *Proceedings of the Prehistoric Society* 53, 419-31.

Wilson, D. 2005. Vertical versus oblique photography. In C. Bacilieri, A. Faustmann, N. Heiska, I. Oltean & L. Żuk (eds), *AARGnews Supplement 1 Festschrift dedicated to Rog Palmer on his 60th birthday.* 32-4.

4

Clays and 'difficult' soils in eastern and southern Scotland: dealing with the gaps

David C. Cowley and Amanda L. Dickson

INTRODUCTION

Sustained observer-directed aerial survey across lowland Scotland has recovered large numbers of plough-levelled archaeological monuments recorded as crop marks on oblique aerial photographs. The vast majority of these sites lie in arable ground, though some have also been recorded as parchmarks in pasture (*10*). The distribution of sites recovered to date is extensive, but it is uneven, and while some of the reasons for variability are relatively clear, such as the overall extent of arable, there are gaps that are less easy to explain. This paper seeks to explore some of the factors that lie behind the variability with a view to establishing the reliability, or otherwise, of the site distributions recovered. This is not only a prerequisite for the archaeological interpretation of the material, but is also a process to critically evaluate survey practice and ensure that it remains effective in exploring the arable (lowland) zone.

THE ARABLE ZONE

For the last half-century and more arable land use in Scotland has been concentrated in the east and south of the country. The better quality and freer drained soils are located in this area, which also benefits from a relatively dry climate. The drop-off in Soil Moisture Deficit (SMD; see Evans; this volume) figures to the west and north of Scotland is very marked and figures of about 100mm are only routinely achieved in easternmost parts.

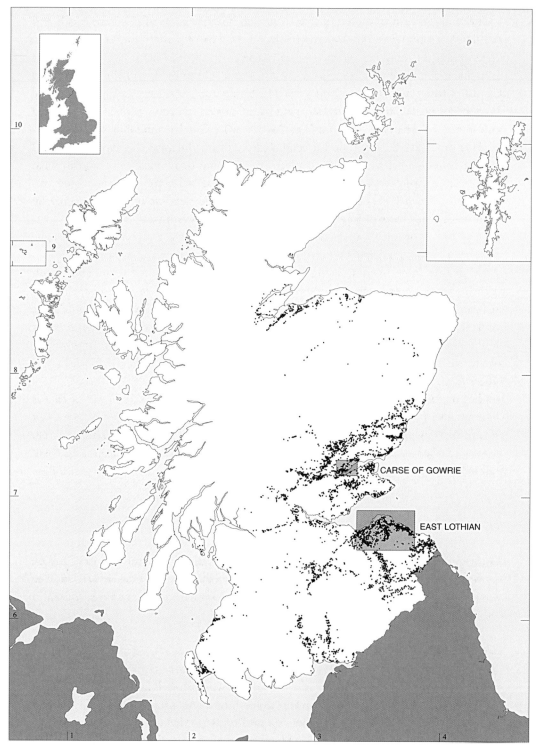

10 The distribution of plough-levelled archaeological sites recorded as crop marks in Scotland up to the end of 2002 and locations referred to in the text. *Crown copyright: RCAHMS*

This combination of factors creates a susceptibility to crop stress in the south and east that has routinely produced crop marks on the sites of plough-levelled monuments. Programmes of observer-directed aerial survey to record them have taken place ever since the 1940s, but principally by the Royal Commission on the Ancient and Historical Monuments of Scotland (RCAHMS) since 1976. To date, the character of the distribution of sites recorded reflects patterns of survey and the extent of well-drained soils in the drier parts of Scotland (e.g. Cowley 2002; Cowley and Gilmour 2005a, illus 24; Hanson 2005). Survey time has tended to focus on the areas that have guaranteed reasonable returns, reinforcing the pattern and creating dense clusters of sites in what have been referred to as 'honey-pots' (Cowley 2002). Beyond the honey-pots, on imperfectly drained, deeper soils and the very localised deposits of clays (certainly by comparison with parts of England), the distributions of sites thin or disappear.

This pattern has developed into a marked contrast between the highly productive honey-pots and significant blocks of lowland ground that have remained stubbornly blank, despite some of these being in the driest areas. This requires explanation, both in terms of the interpretation of the archaeological data and in developing approaches to establish the overall reliability of the survey material. A very basic, but nonetheless fundamental question remains after 30 years of aerial survey, and that is to what extent do the distributions of crop marks reflect earlier settlement and land use in the lowlands, and to what extent do they reflect modern survey strategies imposed uncritically across different types of soil and variable patterns of rainfall?

The robustness, or otherwise, of interpretations that make use of this survey data is determined by the extent to which this question can be addressed. This is also a key issue in identifying the limitations of aerial survey in exploring certain regions, and lays down a challenge to develop other techniques more appropriate to exploring these 'difficult areas'.

CLAYS AND 'DIFFICULT' SOILS

The exploration of these issues in this paper is considered through two case studies: the first dealing with a block of clay-derived soils in the Carse of Gowrie (*11*), and the second looking at the interplay of well-drained and imperfectly drained (i.e. 'difficult') soils in East Lothian (*12*).

Clays: the Carse of Gowrie

This low-lying area on the north bank of the Firth of Tay contains one of these marked contrasts, ranging from complete absence of known archaeological sites, to a dense concentration of monuments, all within a distance of no more than a few hundred metres. The reasons for this have been explored by RCAHMS (1994) and recently re-examined (Dickson 2004). The Carse of Gowrie originates as a bay in the late and post-glacial estuary of the river Tay. The Carse itself is mainly composed of estuarine clays, but around its edge is an old shoreline of raised beach deposits. These are predominantly

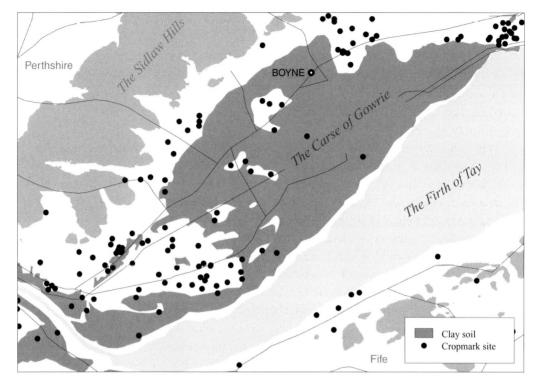

11 The distribution of crop-marked sites in the Carse of Gowrie shown against the generalised extent of clay soils. With the exception of Boyne, the sites that appear to be on the clay are in fact on unmapped gravel ridges. *Crown copyright: RCAHMS*

gleyed, but there are also patches of Brown Forest soils derived from fine sands, silts and gravels coincident with old sandbanks, now forming low ridges, and the raised shorelines are also composed of freely draining gravels. Present land use is dominated by arable, with rotations of root crops and some pasture.

Medieval and later place-names suggest a generally damp environment in the bottom of the Carse, interspersed with slightly drier elevated ridges and knolls. Drainage schemes have undoubtedly altered the character of the area considerably (RCAHMS 1994, 2), but beyond this generalisation, the question remains of when this area was first brought into cultivation and actively settled.

The known distribution (*11*) of plough-levelled sites recorded as crop marks is emphatically on the sands and gravels, a single exception being at Boyne on the clay (other sites that appear to be on the clay are in fact on gravel ridges that are not mapped on the geological maps). This distribution pattern is derived from speculative observer-directed survey, and there is little explicit survey design against which the reliability of the results can be measured. A retrospective examination of the pattern of aerial survey in the region does not help in establishing its reliability, rather it shows all the signs of being conditioned by an emphasis on high returns from the honey-pots, which are largely situated along the raised beach deposits. The Carse of Gowrie has been over flown repeatedly, largely due to the adjacent honey-pots, but also because it lies on a transit route. The detail of the survey pattern suggests that the clay lands of the Carse have not been subjected to the intensive examination that the adjacent gravels have received, and have tended to be ignored during years in which crop-marked information was abundant. In these 'good' years attention has been focused on the honey-pots, where returns have been guaranteed and there is a high incidence of repeat photography of previously known sites (below).

No other complementary datasets are available to help evaluate the reliability of this distribution. Firstly, the area has not benefited from a concerted programme of fieldwalking and the few small finds that exist come from somewhat ambiguous contexts. Secondly, the extensive coverage of vertical aerial photography of the study area, spanning the period between 1946 and 1988, does not include any imagery taken under optimal conditions; even known sites were barely visible, and the coverage cannot be used with any confidence to identify unrecorded monuments.

The study of the Carse of Gowrie throws up a basic paradox in evaluating the reliability of aerial survey across the area. Somewhat limited and ambiguous results hint that site distributions are unreliable. Equally, potentially complementary data are missing, while vertical coverage does little to complement the observer-directed survey as it has been captured in less than ideal conditions. The overall result is that there are only hints that the clay lands here were settled before the medieval period, but this statement is clearly based on a heavily biased dataset. The only recorded archaeological crop mark on the clays, at Boyne, has been interpreted as an Iron Age souterrain (RCAHMS 1994), but the crop marks lack clear definition and the attribution is therefore open to doubt.

'Difficult' soils: East Lothian

Leaving aside the limited areas of clays with their own particular problems, there are significant gaps in distributions of known sites in other areas across the arable lowlands of the eastern seaboard of Scotland, illustrated here with reference to East Lothian (12). These gaps coincide with imperfectly drained soils, which are referred to here as 'difficult' in the sense that they have proved remarkably intractable to aerial survey. This is all the more marked as these areas are amongst the driest in Scotland, are consistently set to arable, and lie close to the main base for RCAHMS aerial survey at Edinburgh airport. They have been surveyed from the air on a yearly basis since 1976, and the overall patterning of sites was established by the early 1980s. Subsequent survey has continued to reveal new sites, but these tend to be within the known clusters of monuments (i.e. the honey-pots), rather than extending the overall distribution.

Thus, the archaeological record is one of marked contrasts between very dense clusters of sites in honey-pots, and significant gaps. Many of these gaps are coterminous with imperfectly drained Brown Forest soils that are essentially fragile and have a tendency towards water-logging. Decades of aerial reconnaissance indicate that these areas are not as likely to produce crop marking as the freely draining soils, an observation that has subsequently been reinforced by survey resources being concentrated into areas of guaranteed return, even if the majority of this return is repeat information. As with the

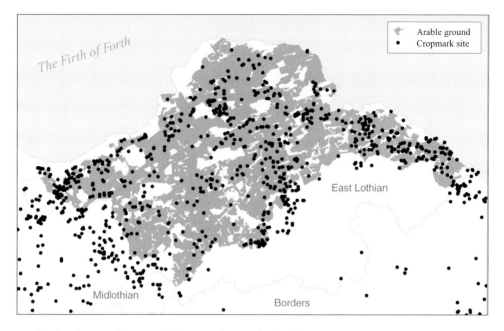

Arable ground
• Cropmark site

12 The distribution of crop-marked sites and generalised arable ground in East Lothian. *Crown copyright: RCAHMS, arable ground in East Lothian derived from MLURI mapping based on 1988 aerial photography*

Carse of Gowrie, this emphasis in aerial survey strategy calls into question the overall reliability of the distribution pattern and how well it reflects past settlement.

A recent illustration of the way in which the honey-pots have tended to attract more attention than the gaps can be seen in the distribution of sites recorded by RCAHMS during 2000 in East Lothian, where about 70% are repeat photography of previously recorded monuments and the minority were previously unrecorded (*13*). The broad pattern of survey work has now changed (below). However, this example illustrates the extent to which the emphasis of aerial survey, since the broad distribution of crop marks was established, has tended to reinforce site distributions rather than challenge them.

However, in contrast to the Carse of Gowrie, there are three complementary data sets that provide a basic means of evaluating the reliability of the survey results in these areas. Firstly, as can be seen in the map of sites recorded in East Lothian during 2000 (*13*), a few of the previously unrecorded sites lie on the edges of clusters of known sites and in the gaps between. This alone indicates that at least parts of the overall distribution are a product of survey strategies.

Secondly, the archaeological evaluation and monitoring in advance of the upgrading of parts of the A1 road to dual carriageway has identified a series of unrecorded monuments (Lelong and MacGregor 2006). Extending from Haddington eastwards, this is the largest scale topsoil stripping and archaeological monitoring in Scotland to date. The road line had been designed to avoid known archaeological sites, which in this area are principally those recorded as crop marks. The results from the project are

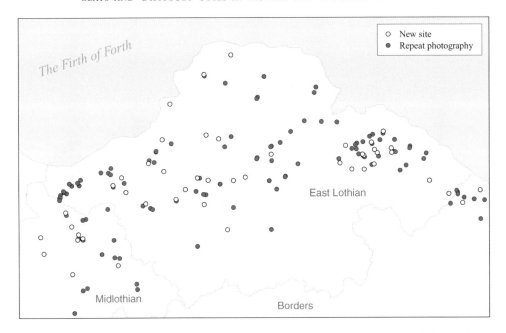

13 The distribution of crop-marked sites recorded during RCAHMS survey in 2000, differentiating between those photographed for the first time in that year and repeat photography of previously known monuments. *Crown copyright: RCAHMS*

interesting as it produced two very different patterns along the narrow corridor of the road line. A large area in the west was completely blank, while to the east a scatter of previously unknown sites were identified. The blank area, which extended over 5.5km and was extensively sampled and closely monitored, lies on imperfectly drained soils. To the east, where the sites were identified, the road line lies on well-drained soils in a swathe of ground that nonetheless had not been productive during aerial survey. The data from the AI project in this case tends to confirm the distribution recovered from aerial survey: expanding the concentration of known sites on the freely drained soils on the one hand, and on the other providing some corroboration that at least one gap may be a real reflection of past activity.

Thirdly, block vertical coverage was photographed during optimal conditions in the summers of 1976 and 1977. These afford extensive views of large swathes of ground without the observer bias of the RCAHMS aerial survey. The assessment of these photographs is work in progress, but early indications suggest that the block coverage will allow the exploration of the validity of some gaps.

In East Lothian the benefits of area mapping and analysis for understanding regional patterning in the data are being felt. At a local scale it can be observed that the few sites recorded on imperfectly drained soils lie on low rises and ridges where the soil is thin, contrasting with the gaps where soil is consistently deeper (see Evans; this volume). At a broader, regional scale, the light shed by mapping and analysis on the pattern of Iron Age pit-defined boundaries is a good case in point (*14*). These sites have been recorded since

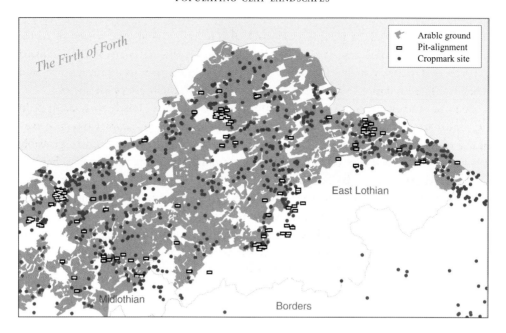

	Arable ground
□	Pit-alignment
•	Cropmark site

14 The distribution of pit-defined boundaries in East Lothian shown against the generalised extent of arable ground and all sites recorded as crop marks. *Crown copyright: RCAHMS, arable ground derived from MLURI mapping based on 1988 aerial photography*

the early years of aerial survey and their discovery led to an expectation that the coastal plain was extensively enclosed by the end of the first millennium BC. However, the assessment of their distribution across the county (*14*) has shown that they are clustered, sometimes concentrating around major hillforts. Furthermore, their disposition is not a random one, as the contrast between the distribution of all crop-marked sites and those of pit-alignments shows. In this case, the distribution recovered by aerial survey probably reflects patterns in later prehistoric economic and political structures. This illustrates the potential of the analysis of regional site distributions to reveal patterns that appear to reflect past activity, rather than survey strategy or the distributions of soils.

'DIFFICULT' SOILS IN SCOTLAND: GENERAL OBSERVATIONS

During the early years of archaeological aerial survey in Scotland effort was concentrated into productive areas that, by and large, have provided the focus for subsequent survey. The overall distribution of plough-levelled sites recorded as crop marks was established in outline by the mid-1980s, though extreme conditions, such as those of 1992, produced significant enhancements of the pattern. After the explosion of previously unrecorded sites during the early years, an expectation of maintaining high returns of sites in order to justify the continuation of the aerial survey programme saw focus maintained on the honey-pot areas, with relatively little effort directed at exploring less responsive, more difficult ground. In part, this approach also reflects a deliberate policy of repeat photography under differing conditions. Overall, however, this pattern of work has created a dataset that, whilst valuable, should carry a health warning over its representativity and reliability. The limitations for areas of difficult soils are all the more pronounced.

The case studies presented above identify two broad patterns. Firstly, there are gaps in site distributions that are most likely to be a product of biases in recovery due to survey practice or local soils. Secondly, there are genuine gaps, such as in East Lothian, probably reflecting ancient practice. Both instances are a reminder that the validity or otherwise of distributions needs to be established, rather than assumed. Here, the perceptions of workers undoubtedly come to bear and these are likely to be strongly influenced by the contemporary landscape. For example, it is a commonplace expectation that upland land use and settlement will be intermittent in time and space, broken by higher ground, bog or other topographic constraints, whereas in lowland areas the contemporary landscape of wall-to-wall fields and dense patterns of settlement informs an expectation of a similar arrangement in the past – certainly by the later prehistoric period. It is worth noting, however, that in many parts of Scotland the enclosure and infilling of the landscape is an artefact of the mid- to late-eighteenth century. The last two centuries of increasingly intensive agriculture have seen watercourses canalised or culverted and micro-topography ironed out as knolls and ridges are eroded and gullies in-filled. The landscape of coterminous and extensive enclosure and settlement that is seen in lowlands such as East Lothian today is not a model to extend back beyond the eighteenth century, though for a twenty-first century set of eyes it is a pervasive one.

Past populations are likely to have recognised intuitively that certain areas may be more suitable for some purposes than others. In this context, settlement and land use patterns throughout the prehistoric period, and probably through the first millennium AD, may well be characterised by discrete clusters of settlement and significant gaps. The care for an archaeologist lies in not extending perceptions derived from a contemporary view into a deterministic model that is driven by simplistic relationships between soils and biased survey data.

APPROACHES TO 'DIFFICULT' SOILS: MAKING SURVEY COUNT

Archaeological aerial survey in Scotland has produced spectacular results, populating large areas with hitherto unrecorded monuments. Over the last 30 years of sustained survey the approach taken by RCAHMS has evolved to take account of changing conditions, drawing on analysis of survey methodology and its results. The focus of activity on the honey-pots that characterised the early years of survey was understandable while large numbers of new sites were being recovered. However, the effectiveness of maintaining this emphasis as the principal component of survey methodology is challenged by both the high incidence of repeat photography of known sites, and the bias in the resulting dataset. As a result RCAHMS aerial survey policy has now developed to emphasise survey of previously less productive areas at the expense of re-recording previously known sites. The challenge lies in developing effective approaches that maximise returns from areas of difficult soils. One aspect of this approach is the recognition that these areas should be prioritised.

In Scotland, this prioritisation is a first step in a necessarily long-term programme to explore the known potential of the areas of difficult soils. The programme will not be reserved for years when extreme weather conditions are producing significant crop stress, and will also target these areas in more typical conditions. The generally damp summers of recent years have not been conducive to crop mark formation, but survey by RCAHMS in 2005 shows the potential returns from such areas even in otherwise mediocre years for crop marking.

The summer of 2005 was generally warm and damp, and followed a wet spring. SMD figures only crept above 100mm in limited areas and crop marking was not widespread. Indeed, many sites that could usually be relied on to show were not visible. However, wide-ranging reconnaissance identified a pattern of discrete areas of crop marking, presumably reflecting local patterns of rainfall, and recovered a high proportion of previously unrecorded monuments. One such area was the West Rhins in the far south-west of Scotland, to the west of the spectacular honey-pot of well-drained soils between Stranraer and Luce Bay (Cowley 2002; Cowley and Brophy 2001). Whereas these well-drained soils were unproductive, the adjacent area to the west produced a good return of predominately new monuments. In addition, sorties directed to record buildings and landscape produced some surprises. For example, the possible prehistoric settlement enclosure at Broom Hill in Renfrewshire (15) was discovered while taking off from Glasgow airport on a sortie to record towns and buildings around the Renfrewshire coast. Indifferent SMD figures of 60-70mm for the area had dulled expectations of any crop marking beyond modern drainage and infilled drains (see Evans; this volume). The crop mark is not spectacular but extends the distribution of potentially later prehistoric settlement into an area about which little is otherwise known; incidentally, it lies on poorly drained non-calcareous gleys. Sites that turn up like this are a caution against assumptions of absence. They remind us of the requirement to test the boundaries in keeping survey methodology keen. Such returns will always be limited, but over time they will help to redress the biases inherent in the lowland site distributions, providing a more reliable base from which to understand the past.

The change in approach at RCAHMS is happening in the face of factors that may come to limit the ability of traditional aerial survey to recover sites. Highly capitalised farms are investing in plant and technology to reduce crop stress, while there has also been a significant reduction in ground set to arable. In Scotland, the extent of arable has been diminishing year on year, dropping by about 20% between 1982 and 2005, by which date it amounted to about 13% of total agricultural land (Scottish Executive 2006). This trend is unlikely to be reversed, and changes in weather patterns with potentially damper summers will exacerbate the situation. In the long-term traditional aerial reconnaissance may become less effective.

In these circumstances it is important to exploit alternative approaches, such as LIDAR. These not only offer the potential to record monuments on well-drained soils, but also to explore areas of difficult soils and permanent pasture, which are less

15 A possible later prehistoric settlement recorded while taking off from Glasgow airport in an area where archaeological crop marks and prehistoric settlement have not previously been recorded. *Crown copyright: RCAHMS, rectified image E60145reGS.tif, photographed 22 July 2005*

responsive to traditional aerial survey. The increasing availability and resolution of satellite imagery should also inform reconnaissance strategies. This type of coverage carries its own limitations, but it could be used to assess the state of crops early in the season (e.g. Cowley and Gilmour 2005b, 58-9), and carries implications for the balance between aerial reconnaissance and desk-based assessment in undertaking aerial survey, in particular if the diminishing returns that are suggested above come to pass. Underpinning this view is alertness to the limitations of observer-directed aerial reconnaissance in creating rounded and reliable datasets (e.g. Oakey 2005; Palmer 2005).

CONCLUSION

Aerial survey in Scotland is continuing to produce valuable results and, with the refinements to its strategy outlined above, should continue to do so for some time to come. However, the question of how long this broad approach will remain appropriate is an important one and will be kept under review. Explicit and accountable survey design, in which aerial reconnaissance, field survey and mapping are integrated, is a key to making aerial survey count (see also Cowley 2005). Fundamentally, the survey process must be responsive to change and should maintain an engagement with what the dots on maps really mean. In the context of the difficult soils and clays in Scotland this lies primarily in identifying the real concentrations and gaps in site distributions that reflect patterning in past activity.

ACKNOWLEDGEMENTS

Our thanks to Olivia Lelong for making the A1 information available in advance of publication, to Strat Halliday, Rebecca Jones and Jack Stevenson for comments on the text, and to Kevin Macleod for producing the maps and rectifying the aerial photograph. Thanks also to Rog and Jess for their patience during editing.

BIBLIOGRAPHY

Cowley, D.C. 2002. A case study in the analysis of patterns of aerial reconnaissance in a lowland area of southwest Scotland. *Archaeological Prospection* 9:4, 255-65.

Cowley, D.C. 2005. Aerial reconnaissance and vertical photography in upland Scotland: integrating the resources. In J. Bourgeois & M. Meganck (eds), *Aerial photography and archaeology 2003 – a century of information*, 67-79. Ghent: Academia.

Cowley, D.C. & Brophy, K. 2001. The impact of aerial photography across the lowlands of south-west Scotland. *Transactions of the Dumfriesshire and Galloway Natural History and Antiquarian Society* 75, 47-72.

Cowley, D.C. & Gilmour, S.M. 2005a. Some observations on the nature of aerial survey. In K. Brophy & D.C. Cowley (eds), *From the air: understanding aerial archaeology*, 50-63. Stroud: Tempus.

Cowley, D.C. & Gilmour, S.M. 2005b. Discovery from the air: a pit-defined cursus monument in Fife. *Scottish Archaeological Journal* 25:2, 171-8.

Dickson, A.L. 2004. *A review of aerial archaeology over the clay soils in the Carse of Gowrie, SE Perthshire*. Unpublished MPhil. University of Glasgow, Department of Archaeology.

Hanson, W.S. 2005. Sun, sand and see: creating bias in the archaeological record. In K. Brophy & D.C. Cowley (eds), *From the air: understanding aerial archaeology*, 73-85. Stroud: Tempus.

Lelong, O. & MacGregor, G. 2006. *Emerging Lothian landscapes: research frameworks and the archaeology of the A1*. Scottish Archaeological Internet Reports, www.sair.org.uk, accessed April 2006.

Oakey, M. 2005. Patterns of aerial photography in the Central Midlands of England – evaluating biases in past programmes of aerial reconnaissance and their potential impact. In K. Brophy & D.C. Cowley (eds), *From the air: understanding aerial archaeology*, 141-50. Stroud: Tempus.

Palmer, R. 2005. If they used their own photographs they wouldn't take them like that. In K. Brophy & D.C. Cowley (eds), *From the air: understanding aerial archaeology*, 94-116. Stroud: Tempus.

RCAHMS, 1994. *South-East Perth an archaeological landscape*, Edinburgh: HMSO.

Scottish Executive, 2006. *Scotland Statistics*. www.scotland.gov.uk/Publications/2006/02/1309212 9/1; www.scotland.gov.uk/library3/environment/afsb-08.asp), accessed April 2006.

5

In pursuit of the invisible: are there crop-marked sites on clay-like soils in Poland?

Grzegorz Kiarszys, Włodzimierz Rączkowski, Lidia Żuk

INTRODUCTION

An archaeologist's knowledge and opinions play a significant role in interpreting past human activities. Most Polish archaeologists do not expect traces of settlements on heavy soils. This assumption has an impact on the practice of fieldwork as well as aerial reconnaissance. Results of aerial reconnaissance during the last few years refute this opinion and numerous features have been identified in a variety of crops growing on a range of soil types. We will present several examples of such sites which appeared on clay-like soils and compare the aerial evidence with results from surface collection.

Even rough analysis of the distribution of archaeological sites shows an irregularity of their arrangement. As a logical course the following question arises: why is it that there are very few or almost no sites in some regions, whereas there are many sites in others? The history of archaeological thought shows that it is mainly theoretical reflection which plays an important role in the process of explanation or interpretation of past phenomena. Thus, another question is justified in the context of the main trend of this publication: is the lack of settlements on heavy soils an effect of conscious decisions made by man in the past or rather a product of the direction of archaeological research resulting from the way archaeologists think about the past? In this chapter we would like to emphasise the latter trend, i.e. to show how theoretical reflection affects archaeologists' decisions.

David Clarke (1968), analysing the condition of British archaeology in the 1960s (i.e. culture-historical archaeology), described it as 'chaotically unsystematic, undisciplined, intuitive and empirical'. Concerning Polish archaeology of the last few decades this description is still up to date, and even merits the addition of a few more words such as 'inconsistent and full of paradoxes'. These weaknesses are clearly noticeable in the attitude to the relations between settlement patterns and soils (e.g. Rączkowski 1997). A widespread view of the influence of soil types on settlement patterns considers that traces of prehistoric activity in Poland will be concentrated on areas of light, sandy soils which cover some 25% of the country. Map analyses of the distribution of archaeological sites definitely refute this kind of view.

For this paper it is essential to identify what are heavy (or clay-like) soils in Poland. The main factor in the formation of a soil layer is its bedrock. In Poland there are many different kinds of Pleistocene drift which show an extraordinary variability of stratification, granulation, mineral composition etc. They were transported from the north by a Scandinavian glacier. Ground moraine drifts (i.e. talus clays) are most frequent among these formations. They appear in many different varieties – ranging from very heavy to sandy soils – depending on local geomorphological processes which took place in the late Pleistocene and Holocene. On such bedrock there developed eutric cambisols, dystric cambisols and luvisols. Different levels in their profile can include clay sands, strong clay sands, light clays, medium clays and heavy clays, silt and silty clay loam in various proportions. Soils composed in this way cover more than half of Poland (Bednarek & Prusinkiewicz 1999, 185-205).

Sands and gravels build different geomorphological structures due to the effects of glaciations (e.g. terminal moraine). Light soils such as cambic arenosols, albic arenosols, cambic podzols and podzols developed on these structures. These kinds of soil cover about 26% of the area of Poland. The other types of soil occur occasionally, are often dispersed and do not play any significant role in our considerations.

An important element which characterises the soil in Poland is the structure of its dispersion. Patchy (16) and 'multi-component' arrangements are the most common. They consist of various types of blended soils which occupy only small or localised areas which are not marked on the generalised soil maps of 1:300,000 or 1:500,000 scales (Bednarek & Prusinkiewicz 1999, 217-27). Thus, these small areas of black soils, podzols etc., which can be critical in the process of interpretation of settlement patterns, are not taken into analysis/consideration.

This lack of detail in the way in which soils and geologies are mapped in Poland may certainly be an obstacle in all kinds of analyses of settlement patterns, especially from the point of view of an individual archaeological site. However, it does not prevent Polish archaeologists from making generalisations regarding observed spatial distributions and drawing far-reaching conclusions.

'SOILS' IN ARCHAEOLOGICAL INTERPRETATIONS

The issue of the role of soil conditions in past cultures first appeared in archaeological literature at the end of the nineteenth century together with theoretical concepts originating from anthropogeography (e.g. Daniel 1978; Trigger 1989). Actually, inspirations of that type led towards diffusionism and drew attention to the role of space in past

16 An example area showing 'patchy' structure. This is a dominant pattern of soils in Poland

0   500 m

societies. A map became an important research tool to describe and explain cultural phenomena. Among the many different components presented on maps and treated as affecting cultural processes were soils. Their variability was supposed to have an important impact on the ways in which people settled the landscape.

The persuasiveness of maps, especially those ones which present the relations between soil types and settlement patterns, led to the popularisation of such analytical methods. In turn, this led archaeologists to consolidate their views on the dependence of past settlements upon environmental conditions (which led to environmental determinism). Thus, this approach found its place as a fully accepted method in cultural-historical archaeology, which is the synthesis of various inspirations originating from evolutionism and diffusionism.

Since that time analyses of settlement patterns, agricultural developments and cultural change and their relations to types of soil have become standard methods. In most archaeological works, which were published in the twentieth century, the analysis of soil took the key position in the discussions on habitation, exploitation and abandonment processes in some regions. This often resulted in 'soil determinism'.

One of the most spectacular examples of this deeply consolidated view among archaeologists is the presumed relation between the directions of expansion of the Linear Band Pottery Culture (*Linearbandkeramik – LBK*) in Europe in the Early Neolithic and the distribution of loess soils (e.g. Tabaczyński 1970; Hensel & Tabaczyński 1978). This view of the relations between types of soil, cultivation methods and settlement patterns led to the belief that soils which were difficult to cultivate (i.e. heavy soils) were not interesting to the farming communities of Europe for a long period of time. Thus, no traces of settlements on the areas where such soils occur should be expected. So it is obvious that such opinions have a very important influence on research in Polish archaeology. And paradoxically, the empirical evidence indicating the location of Early Neolithic settlements on clay-like soils does not change this opinion (e.g. Czerniak 1994; Kukawka 1997).

FIELDWALKING ON CLAY-LIKE SOILS

Settlement pattern studies, developed intensively since the beginning of the 1960s, promoted the consolidation of such 'soil deterministic' opinions in Polish archaeology. They were focused on studies of environmental conditions of past settlements, especially of relations between climate, surface topography, soil types, hydrological systems and the distribution of archaeological sites. This was a result of the following assumptions (Kruk 1973; Kurnatowski 1963):

1. that natural conditions determined human activities – hence recognition of the confines set by the natural environment allowed archaeologists to specify the directions of economic development of past societies;
2. that settlement process consisted of occupying the most advantageous areas, not in the adaptation to generally less friendly conditions. Consistently, the areas to be settled first were regions with fertile soils that were easily cultivated with simple but very effective tools. Such conditions could be found in river valleys, where light black soils and histosols occurred;
3. that the lack of big settlements in certain regions (upland and watershed areas) indicates that past communities were not interested in them, or exploited them in a very limited way;
4. that the lack of interest in exploitation of heavy soils was the result of technical inability to cultivate them.

From the above points it was accepted that until the thirteenth century settlements concentrated in river valleys, on areas of histosols, light black soils and albic arenosols reaching not much beyond the river valleys. Only technological developments allowed people to settle down and extensively cultivate the upland that was covered mainly with heavy soils (Kurnatowski 1963; 1966). Thus no traces of earlier settlements should be expected in such regions.

Fieldwalking survey as developed by Józef Kostrzewski in the 1920s and 1930s became the principal research method of settlement pattern studies in Poland. This tradition identified the necessity to concentrate surveys along river valleys as settlement location in the past was determined by access to water (impact of environmental determinism). The modification of fieldwalking survey in the 1960s included the requirement to explore all regions including areas beyond the river valleys. However, the precision of investigation was less accurate during surveys carried out on these upland areas (Kruk 1969). The following assumptions formed the basis of research into settlement studies of sites that had been identified by fieldwalking survey:

1. that identical and objective factors (i.e. mainly natural) affect all sites, hence the archaeological material brought to the surface is representative for all buried features;
2. that the quantity of the material indicates the size of the site − numerous fragments of ceramic indicate a vast site, whereas a few sherds signal a small number of archaeological features;
3. that the size of the site is a derivative of its function − large sites mean stable settlements connected with intensive exploitation of the environment, whereas small sites are the manifestation of short stays by human groups (traces of camps).

These assumptions were the basis of the Polish Archaeological Record (*Archeologiczne Zdjęcie Polski – AZP*) programme, a national project which recorded archaeological sites identified by fieldwalking survey (Konopka 1981, 29-30; cf. Barford 2000). The main purpose of *AZP* was to provide uniform recognition of archaeological sites throughout the whole of Poland. In practice, the whole country was mechanically divided into *AZP* working areas (32-35sq km each), which were to be surveyed as a whole, independent of anything that previously had been recorded (Kempisty *et al.* 1981, 23-4; Woyda 1981, 14). For each site a detailed Archaeological Site Register File (*KESA*) was completed. The card designed for the *AZP* programme was a questionnaire of enquiries resulting from the approach to settlement pattern studies that was characteristic at that time. More than half of the sections referred to the detailed description of the environmental context of a site. Soil observations were also taken into consideration. In that section three basic categories were distinguished: sandy soil, clay-like soil and peat-marsh/histosols. Another section was devoted to specifying the stoniness of the soil (ODZ 1981, 47). Thus, it seemed that there was a lot of effort to ensure unbiased and balanced recognition of the actual distribution of archaeological sites in Poland which also took into consideration the possibility of recording them on heavy soils. Did this lead to a revolution in the presentation of past settlements?

In 1996 a collection of papers was published summarising results of the first 15 years of *AZP*. By that time field-walkers had registered archaeological sites over 75% of the country (Jaskanis 1996, 9). Thus, we can assume that the archaeologists' opinions in that book constitute, to some extent, a representative account of views concerning archaeological sites on heavy soils. According to project designers' predictions, fieldwalking surveys caused a rapid increase of information about archaeological sites, changing radically the knowledge of their number and distribution within Poland (Jaskanis 1996, 36). However, it is difficult to find any information on the changes of opinions about the settlements on clay-like soils. These opinions were not even altered after the discovery of a significant number of Neolithic sites on clay-like soils at Ziemia Chełmińska (Sosnowski 1996).

A fundamental question can be asked: why did such a change of view not take place? Certainly, there are a lot of reasons which will be examined by analysing two small sample areas (2km x 2km) from the south of Wielkopolska (Krzywiń vicinity). Both areas are parts of two neighbouring *AZP* working areas: 61-26 and 62-27. Our basic task was to identify the degree of consistency of the description of soil features made by an archaeologist during fieldwalking survey at the stage of filling the *KESA* compared with the 1:10,000 scale soil map. In both areas significant discrepancies were noticed between the soil type specified on the card and that on the soil map. None of the sites discovered in the *AZP* 61-26 working area has been defined as located on clay-like soils but the soil map located eleven of them on clay-like soils (*17 & 18*). At nine sites field descriptions matched those on the soil map. In the *AZP* 62-27 working area, nineteen sites were registered (*19 & 20*). Eleven sites have proper soil definitions, and out of the total number, six sites were defined as located on clay-like soils but only three of them are really on clay-like soils (the remainder are on loose sand).

It is difficult to draw definitive conclusions from that short list although some comments can be made. It is clear that archaeologists' definitions of soil type (even in such generalised categories) are very intuitive and that their individual knowledge, experience and views play a key role. In the *AZP* 62-27 working area fieldwalking survey was carried out by an archaeologist whose speciality was Early Neolithic settlements, so he was aware that there might have been traces of settlements on clay-like soils (especially Neolithic settlements). The type of soil is usually defined on the basis of a surface layer. The estimation of sandiness and clayeyness of the soil depends also on 'the difficulties in walking on it' and the commonly accepted criterion is 'soil stickiness'. So, if the soil does not stick to shoes, it means that it is sandy, and when it sticks just a little bit, the soil is sandy-clay-like. This criterion, however, does not explain what to do when the soil is dry!

Direct physical experience (heavy, soil-coated shoes) 'informs us' about the type of soil we deal with and affects the approach of an archaeologist during fieldwalking survey. When we enter a field with clay-like soil we immediately recall the knowledge that 'I cannot expect' an archaeological site here, although some archaeologists dealing with the Neolithic know differently. As a result a field walker's concentration may be reduced and their perception and recognition of artifacts may be limited. Entering an area of sandy soils evokes quite the opposite reaction – 'there should be something here'. Then the concentration and accuracy of recognition are higher and as a result more archaeological sites are found represented by rich collections of sherds of pottery.

This kind of approach can also be found in numerous publications on settlement systems. Authors of the *AZP* project 'did not expect' to discover any remains of settlements in areas outside of river valleys as these zones frequently comprise heavy soils (Woyda 1981, 14-15).

The idea to carry out investigations on uplands and watershed areas was mainly caused by the belief that all traces indicating any activities connected with environment exploitation

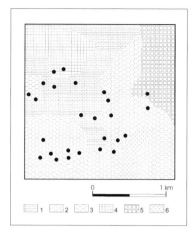
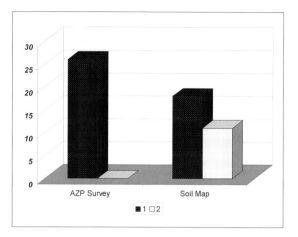

Above left: 17 Fragment of *AZP* 61-26 working area showing the distribution of archaeological sites against bedrock structure. Considerably large patches of light loamy sand covering clay were intuitively and incorrectly defined as sands during fieldwalking survey. Legend: 1 – light loamy sand; 2 – slightly loamy sand; 3 – slightly loamy sand on clay; 4 – heavy loamy sand; 5 – histosols; 6 – woodland

Above right: 18 A comparison of soil descriptions derived from the Archaeological Site Recording Form (*KESA*) and a soil map for the fragment of *AZP* 61-26 working area. The results of *AZP* survey indicate that all sites were located on sandy soils, while the soil map suggests a more balanced picture. Legend: 1 – sandy soils; 2 – clay-like soils

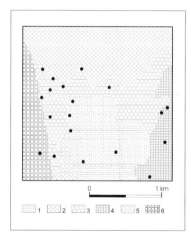
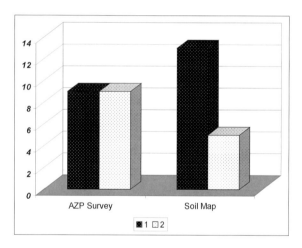

Above left: 19 Fragment of *AZP* 62-27 working area showing the distribution of archaeological sites against bedrock structure. One may notice a comparatively even-numbered dispersion of archaeological sites on different types of soils. Legend: 1 – light loamy sand; 2 – sandy clay loam; 3 – slightly loamy sand; 4 – sand; 5 – woodland; 6 – histosols

Above right: 20 A comparison of a soil description derived from the Archaeological Site Recording Form (*KESA*) and a soil map for the fragment of *AZP* 62-27 working area. Like Figure 3, this statistic also demonstrates that the results of *AZP* survey were determined by the research preferences of an archaeologist in charge. In this case these were in favour of clay-like soils. Legend: 1 – sandy soils; 2 – clay-like soils should be registered (Kruk 1970, 449; Kurnatowski 1974, 552; Woyda 1981, 15). However, no one was expecting any long-term settlement there. It seems that such opinions, and practical solutions originating from them, have deep roots in diffusionism, and especially in archaeologists' acceptance of the essential role of natural factors in cultural changes.

CLAY-LIKE SOILS AND PLANNING ARCHAEOLOGICAL AERIAL RECONNAISSANCE IN POLAND

Definition of the size and function of a site is important for archaeologists carrying out settlement studies. Current practice, which uses information about the quantity of the material collected from the surface for that purpose, raises more and more doubts (e.g. Rączkowski 2005a and see below). Air photographs provide possibilities to overcome existing limitations and it can be assumed that they will also enable a new and different look at the issue of the roles of heavy soils in settlement studies. However, the following question can be put: does 'soil determinism' have also an influence on the planning of aerial reconnaissance in Poland? At present the answer is equivocal because of the small scale (regarding time and space) of such reconnaissance that has been undertaken to date (cf. Rączkowski 2005a; 2005b; Kobyliński 2005). However, this kind of influence indirectly exists.

AERIAL SURVEY IN PRACTICE

One thing that aerial survey can do more extensively and rapidly than any other means of prospection is record plans of buried archaeological features that cannot be identified as such on the ground. This, it seems, has yet to be appreciated by most Polish archaeologists.

In recent years four kinds of archaeological air reconnaissance can be distinguished in Poland. The different approaches depend on the kind of targets requested by the person giving the order, the financial budget, and also, to a high degree, the knowledge (or rather the lack of knowledge – e.g. Rączkowski 2005b) about the potential of aerial survey. The most common reason for taking aerial photographs is to record sites already known from fieldwalking survey, which are of interest to archaeologists and might be excavated in the future. For this, reconnaissance is made along a route from one archaeological site to the next one with photographs being taken of the places where the archaeological sites are located regardless of whether anything is visible or not.

The second kind of reconnaissance takes place along the routes of finished or partly constructed developments such as pipelines or highways. A frequent target of such reconnaissance is the documentation of the process of excavations. Sometimes it is expected that aerial photographs will provide a view of the complete extent of a site of which only a part lies within the corridor and has, perhaps, already been excavated. New sites can be found during this kind of reconnaissance and include the Early Neolithic settlement at Radojewice (Czerniak et al. 2003).

The third kind of reconnaissance is a survey financed (usually) by heritage services in particular regions. The party commissioning the survey usually does not determine any particular aims and allows aerial reconnaissance to operate where and when the observer/photographer chooses. This is more likely to give rise to innovative practice and has the potential to provide the best results. Sometimes an archaeology inspector requests that new photographs include a few places of special importance to them. Most often these are known medieval strongholds.

Finally there is aerial reconnaissance carried out by amateur archaeologists and pilots (e.g. Maciejewski & Rączkowski 2002). They sometimes co-operate with archaeologists and take photographs at their request, but good contacts have to be made to ensure that this may happen. Using the opportunity of flying 'for fun' they may take photographs of landscapes and archaeological sites.

The assumption of the significance of soil type for the development of settlement patterns has the strongest influence on the planning of the third kind of aerial reconnaissance. An important condition of the reconnaissance commissioned by heritage services is to ensure that it is completed efficiently. With only modest means at our disposal (most often for 5–10 flight hours per year) an efficient usage must be presented in reports. How then can such flights be planned? It seems to be simple. First, the flight must be planned in such a way that on the route of the flight there are known medieval strongholds as this will guarantee aerial photographs of archaeological sites (nobody is interested if they bring any new information). The second factor is the choice of regions with numerous sites registered by the *AZP* survey. This factor increases the probability that 'something' can be photographed (an Early Neolithic settlement in Zelgno was photographed on such an occasion (Czerniak *et al.* 2003). Thus, the flights are mainly planned along river valleys. During such reconnaissance a fortified settlement in Jurkowo was discovered (Nowakowski & Rączkowski 2000). Only occasionally during such flights is it possible to divert attention to examine areas of heavy soils, and then it is only in such regions where archaeological sites are known (from incidental discoveries, fieldwalking surveys or excavations). Only in the case of excessive financial means and time (that practically means never) regions 'unsuitable for habitation in the past' are taken into consideration. In the remaining situations the preliminary, tacit assumptions of 'soil determinism' do not play any important role. It is unlikely, therefore, that there will be any significant changes in the existing situation and that regions of clay-like soils will continue not to be considered in any plans of investigation. However, despite the apparent lack of interest, some archaeological sites have been identified during aerial survey over clay-like soils. Some examples of these are considered next.

ANYTHING MIGHT HAPPEN — SOME EXAMPLES

As it has been mentioned above, the experience of Polish aerial archaeology is not very wide. Nevertheless, we can present a few examples where crop-marked archaeological features have been recorded on heavy soils at locations where sites were previously known from *AZP* surveys (*21*).

Krzywiń region

In 1998 a workshop of aerial archaeology was held in Leszno (Barford 1998). At the preparation stage, Otto Braasch, an experienced aerial surveyor who was responsible for the 'air school', asked the organisers to supply him with soil maps. However, use of them was impossible because the maps available at that time were too general to be useful in any way. This example shows that knowledge of the locations of soil types is a usual first step in the planning of aerial reconnaissance in other parts of Europe. On the other hand, the lack of maps ensured that the workshop's reconnaissance was not planned in accordance with the distribution of soil types. However, the presence of river valleys (the Odra, the Obra, and the Barycz rivers) played a certain role in directing the reconnaissance carried out at that time. During the workshop flights, little reference was made to sites known from the *AZP* survey. Instead, all features identified from the air were photographed and reconnaissance routes were completely flexible, allowing flights over any parts of the landscape in the vicinity of Leszno airfield. Sites were photographed in river valleys and in other locations and the results had identified new sites as well as some that had been previously registered. One of the intensively photographed regions in July 1998 was the region of Krzywiń upon the Obra River which provided material that was later used in a Master's Thesis (Kiarszys 2004).

As well as air photographs, data from fieldwalking surveys were also used in the thesis. Aerial photographs were used as an additional source of information to that which came from the *AZP* survey. This enabled comparison of the two methods and allowed analysis of the similarities and discrepancies produced by each. These discrepancies referred mainly to information connected with spatial structures on the sites. The locations of the sites identified on aerial photographs were not always the same as those resulting from fieldwalking surveys. Aerial photographs could also better define the extent of a site. For example, two *AZP* sites situated next to one another turned out to be elements of a bigger feature and should, therefore, be treated as one whole. There were also cases when settlement structures revealed by crop marks had been presented in *AZP* documentation as two separate sites because there was a contemporary road going between them. (This issue is discussed in more detail in Kiarszys 2005; see also Nowakowski *et al.* 1999.)

New sites, which had not been revealed by the *AZP* survey and included some on clay-like soils, were also discovered during aerial reconnaissance. In those cases the aerial view provided the impetus to carry out extra fieldwalking surveys which proved the existence of archaeological material in those fields. An example of this is Krzywiń, site 106, a site on clay-like soils. It was discovered during aerial reconnaissance in 1998 (*22*) at a site where *AZP* surveys carried out in 1981 had not registered any cultural material. In 2003, a fieldwalking survey was carried out on the basis of aerial photographs and produced fragments of ceramic dated to the late Middle Ages and modern period. A similar example is Czerwona Wieś, site 57. It is also situated on clay soil and was revealed by crop marks of archaeological features in 1998.

Another site was located on heavy soils near the village Czerwona Wieś. (In Poland a site recorded on an aerial photograph as crop marks cannot be listed before at least one piece of pottery is found. This is why this site does not have a reference number.)

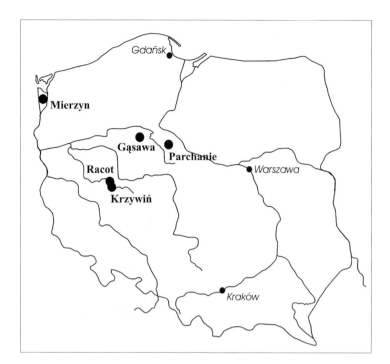

21 Location of sites
discussed in the text

22 Krzywiń, Wielkopolska, site 106. Aerial photograph of a site which was not discovered during *AZP* survey in 1983. However, more careful fieldwalking survey in 2003, guided by the aerial photograph interpretation, yielded several sherds of pottery there. *Photograph: R. Kraujalis, 8.07.1998*

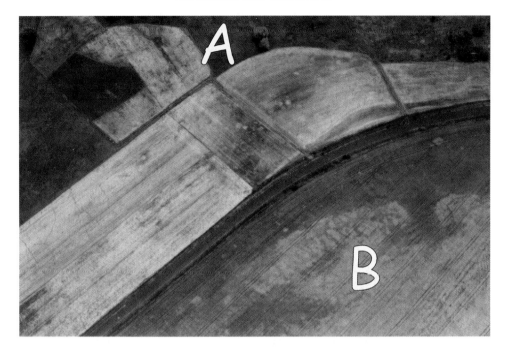

23 Teklimyśl, Wielkopolska, site 86. Aerial photograph of a site with crop marks on histosols (zone A) and clay-like soil (zone B). *Photograph: R. Bewley, 3.07.1998*

Aerial photographs recorded many crop marks of archaeological features in that area demonstrating that it must have been intensively populated in the past. Fieldwalking surveys carried out over the site in 2003 did not provide any archaeological material. The clarity of the crop-marked information suggests that the archaeological features below them have not yet been erased by ploughing. Indeed, the site and its artefacts may be unusually well protected by a comparatively thick layer of topsoil. Similarly protected crop-marked sites have been investigated elsewhere (Connor and Palmer 2000).

Another example is Teklimyśl, site 86. In 1998 crop marks of archaeological features (pits) were photographed on both sides of the road (*23*). The site was discovered during an *AZP* survey in 1979 but was known only on one side of the road (zone A). Fieldwalking surveys from 2003 proved the presence of the archaeological material in accordance with the conclusions drawn from photo analysis thus confirming that the site was spread across both sides of the modern road, too (zone B). The surface finds included Neolithic, Roman, Iron Age, Early Medieval, Late Medieval and modern pottery. Comparison of the location of the site with a soil map showed that the part of the site located in zone A lies on histosols whereas the part which was unknown earlier (zone B) is on clay-like soils.

Mierzyn

Site 5 in Mierzyn was identified for the first time in 1937, however during the next survey carried out in 1983 within the *AZP* programme no traces of archaeological

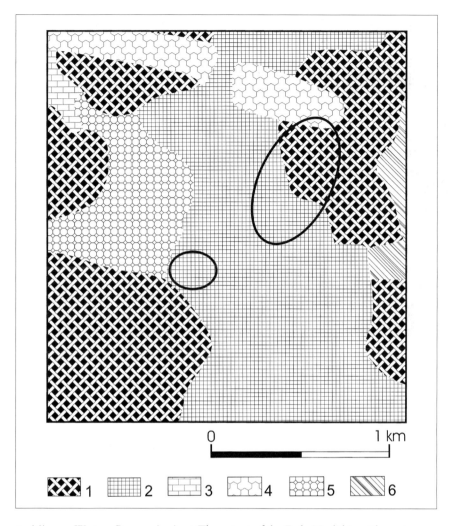

24 Mierzyn, Western Pomerania, site 5. The extent of the Early Neolithic settlements was determined on the basis of the aerial photograph interpretation and shown against a soil map. This example demonstrates that despite prevailing views on the lack of Neolithic sites on heavy soils, aerial photography allows us to record traces of intensive and long-term habitation there. Legend: 1 – light loam; 2 – silty light loam; 3 – light loamy sand; 4 – slightly loamy sand; 5 – sand; 6 – built-up area

material were noticed other than one flint chip. This was found some distance from site 5 and was registered as site 12. The lithic discovery suited the traditional views regarding dispersion of archaeological sites as it was found on clay-like soils (*24*) (described correctly on *KESA*), where it was considered justified to expect only short-term habitation (e.g. camps) such as a single flint chip may indicate.

Around 1996, a development trench was cut across the area of site 5. During small-scale rescue excavations large, well-preserved Neolithic features were found. These persuaded the archaeologists carrying out the investigation to examine existing aerial photographs. These showed a large area to be densely packed with pits, which almost certainly remained from earlier human activity and showed that the site was probably a vast settlement (Dziewanowski & Żuk 2005). The extended area of the site as identified on aerial photographs, plus a smaller outlier to the south-west, is shown in figure (*24*).

To understand the differences in the identification of a site presented by fieldwalking survey and aerial photographs, it was necessary to assess the numbers of archaeological artifacts found in each pit. Out of the nine pits discovered in the trench, the finds totalled only one fragment of pottery and one flint chip. All were below 0.4m beneath the plough soil. With such a low density of archaeological material even deep ploughing would not have revealed much. On the one hand this shows why such a site was overlooked during fieldwalking survey, but on the other it demonstrates that attempts to categorise the function of a site on the basis of the collected surface material simply miss the target.

Gąsawa

The fortified lake-side village at Biskupin is an icon of Polish archaeology (see Kostrzewski 1938). Intensive archaeological studies have been carried out in its region since the mid 1930s, so it is not surprising that the whole area is well recognised. However it is paradoxical that Biskupin, associated with the spectacular beginnings of aerial photography in Poland, has never been an object of a systematic aerial survey. In 2005, in response to a request by the Archaeological Museum in Biskupin, one reconnaissance flight took place. During the flight, photographs of a few sites were taken but the results were far from what was expected. Among the photographed sites on clay-like soils there was a large settlement (Gąsawa, site 5) that was visible as a concentration of crop-marked pits (*25*). In discussion about this site during analysis of the photographs, it was noted that vegetational differences were often visible on the ground in the summer. On that basis archaeological features were located and trial excavations were carried out (Anna Grossmann – pers. comm.).

Kujawy region

Kujawy was a region of very intensive habitation in the past. Because of this it has been of interest to archaeologists for many years. Recently, a rather un-systematic programme of aerial reconnaissance was carried out there by W. Stępień and W. Rączkowski. Since 2000, aerial reconnaissance has brought wonderful results in this area and the archaeologists studying Kujawy's past use the new method more and more willingly. In 2005, quite a new idea was born – to make an aerial survey of a certain area before the *AZP* fieldwalking took place. Thus, in July 2005 one flight was carried out during which the chosen area was thoroughly investigated. Within one hour and a half over 50 sites were photographed, including three impressive Early Neolithic settlements with trapezoidal long houses. The numbers and types of site were very pleasing to the aerial surveyors and made an excellent demonstration of what could be achieved during one short flight over unknown territory. Moreover, looking happily at the photographs of two sites with long houses (Słońsko) they shook their heads with disbelief – 'These settlements cannot be there'. The answer to the question, 'Why?' was, 'There are no proper soils there'. Two sites are on sandy soils, but the third of those Neolithic settlements (Parchanie) lies on heavy soils (*26*).

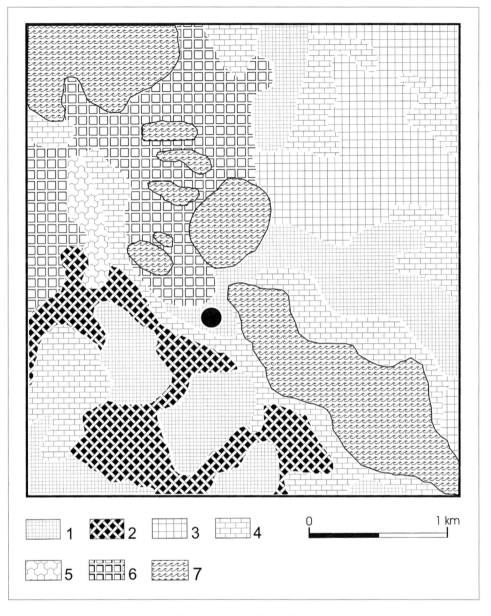

25 Gąsawa, Pałuki, site 5. Location of a site shown against soil distribution. Legend: 1 – silty light loam; 2 – light loam; 3 – heavy loamy sand; 4 – light loamy sand; 5 – slightly loamy sand; 6 – histosols; 7 – lakes

Racot and Białcz Stary

Results are not always so good in this region. Fairly regular aerial reconnaissance has been carried out near Leszno for almost ten years. Different sites have been photographed but almost every flight passes over two known Neolithic settlements at Białcz Stary and Racot (south Wielkopolska). Both sites have been excavated to a small

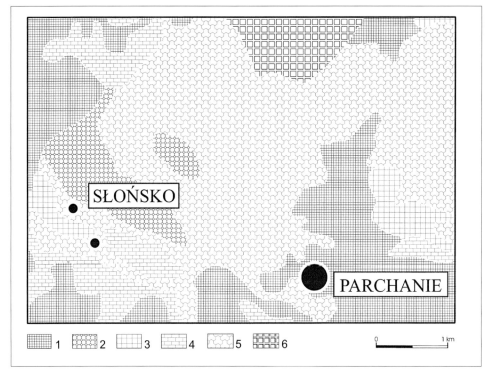

26 Parchanie and Słońsko, Kujawy. Location of early Neolithic settlements shown against soil distribution. Legend: 1 – silty light loam; 2 – sand; 3 – heavy loamy sand; 4 – light loamy sand; 5 – slightly loamy sand; 6 – histosols

degree and long houses have been identified. Both sites are located on areas with heavy soils. Neither long houses nor any other archaeological features have yet been revealed by crop marks.

CONCLUSIONS

Summarising our considerations on the studies of populating clay-like soils, it is clear that archaeologists' knowledge and opinions play a significant role in interpreting past human activities (see the impact of pre-understanding on research – e.g. Hodder 1999; Rączkowski 2005a). There is a common belief that heavy soils are difficult to cultivate and could only be farmed and permanently inhabited after reaching a certain level of technology (clearly evolutionary thinking). This opinion is deeply rooted and functions as a scientific myth. Hence it has an important impact on trends of our research and ways of interpretations.

We cannot deny the influence of another opinion (at least among Polish archaeologists) that the same objective factors influence the identification of archaeological sites on the surface through the presence of pieces of pottery. The fact that post-depositional processes can proceed in different ways depending on various soil conditions (e.g. erosion rate, topsoil thickness, depth of ploughing etc.) is not yet taken into consideration.

A similar situation refers to the presence of archaeological crop marks on clay-like soils. Here, the processes of the development of crop marks may be different to those which influence their development on light soils. Further studies considering this should be undertaken as in this case it seems that the previous negative views were passed directly to aerial archaeology. As a result it seems to be a justified statement that the 'absence' of settlements on clay-like soils in the past is due more to 'limitations' of our research practice (theories, methods) than to the reluctance of past people to settle down in 'difficult' conditions.

BIBLIOGRAPHY

Barford, P. 1998. Reflections on the Leszno aerial archaeology school. *AARGnews* 17, 29-30.

Barford, P. 2000. The Polish Archaeological Record, www.muzarp.poznan.pl/archweb/archweb_eng/barf.htm (accessed April 2006).

Bednarek, R. & Prusinkiewicz, Z. 1999. *Geografia gleb*. Warszawa: Wydawnictwo Naukowe PWN.

Clarke, D. 1968. *Analytical archaeology*. London: Methuen.

Connor, A. & Palmer, R. 2000. An Iron Age ditched enclosure system at Limes Farm, Landbeach, Cambridgeshire. *Antiquity* 74, 281-82.

Czerniak, L. 1994. *Wczesny i środkowy okres neolitu na Kujawach*. Poznań: Polska Akademia Nauk, Instytut Archeologii i Etnologii.

Czerniak, L., Rączkowski, W. & Sosnowski, W. 2003. New prospects for the study of Early Neolithic longhouses in the Polish Lowlands. *Antiquity* 77 http://antiquity.ac.uk/ProjGall/czerniak/czerniak.html (accessed April 2006).

Daniel, G. 1978. *A hundred and fifty years of archaeology*. London: Duckworth.

Dziewanowski, M. & Żuk, L. 2005. Zaległości „nie do odrobienia"? Przyczynek do przydatności zdjęć lotniczych w badaniach terenowych na przykładzie stan. 5 w Mierzynie, woj. zachodniopomorskie. In J. Nowakowski, A. Prinke & W. Rączkowski (eds), *Biskupin … i co dalej? Zdjęcia lotnicze w polskiej archeologii*, 327-35. Poznań: Wydawnictwo AdRem.

Hensel, W. & Tabaczyński, S. 1978. *Rewolucja neolityczna i jej znaczenie dla rozwoju kultury europejskiej*. Wrocław: Ossolineum.

Hodder, I. 1999. *The archaeological process: an introduction*. Oxford: Blackwell.

Jaskanis, D. 1996. Próba oceny metody archeologicznego zdjęcia Polski na podstawie doświadczeń ogólnokrajowego koordynatora. In D. Jaskanis (ed.), *Archeologiczne Zdjęcie Polski – metoda i doświadczenia. Próba oceny*, 9-38. Warszawa: Ministerstwo Kultury i Sztuki.

Kempisty, A., Kruk, J., Kurnatowski, S., Mazurowski, R., Okulicz, J., Rysiewska, T. & Woyda, S. 1981. Projekt założeń metodyczno – organizacyjnych archeologicznego zdjęcia ziem polskich. In M. Konopka (ed.), *Zdjęcie Archeologiczne Polski*, 22-27. Warszawa: Ministerstwo Kultury i Sztuki, Generalny Konserwator Zabytków.

Kiarszys, G. 2004. *Społeczne konstruowanie i organizacja przestrzeni we wczesnym średniowieczu na przykładzie mikroregionu Krzywiń*, Unpublished MA thesis, Poznań.

Kiarszys, G. 2005. Osadnictwo czy krajobraz kulturowy: konsekwencje poznawcze korelacji wyników badań powierzchniowych i rozpoznania lotniczego. In J. Nowakowski, A. Prinke & W. Rączkowski (eds), *Biskupin … i co dalej? Zdjęcia lotnicze w polskiej archeologii*, 389-95. Poznań: Wydawnictwo AdRem.

Kobyliński, Z. 2005. *Archeologia lotnicza w Polsce. Osiem dekad wzlotów i upadków*, Warszawa: PMA, IAiE PAN.

Konopka, M. 1981. Problem wdrożenia programu „zdjęcia archeologicznego" w Polsce – koncepcja realizacji. In M. Konopka (ed.), *Zdjęcie Archeologiczne Polski*, 28-39. Warszawa: Ministerstwo Kultury i Sztuki, Generalny Konserwator Zabytków.

Kostrzewski, J. 1938. Biskupin: an Early Iron Age village in Western Poland. *Antiquity* 12, 311-17.

Kruk, J. 1969. Badania poszukiwawcze i weryfikacyjne w dorzeczu Dłubni. *Sprawozdania Archeologiczne* 21, 347-73.

Kruk, J. 1970. Z zagadnień metodyki badań terenowych. *Sprawozdania Archeologiczne* 22, 445-56.

Kruk, J. 1973. *Studia osadnicze nad neolitem wyżyn lessowych.* Wrocław, Warszawa, Kraków, Gdańsk: Zakład Narodowy imienia Ossolińskich, Wydawnictwo Polskiej Akademii Nauk.

Kukawka, S. 1997. *Na rubieży środkowoeuropejskiego świata wczesnorolniczego: społeczności ziemi chełmińskiej w IV tysiącleciu p.n.e.* Toruń: Uniwersytet Mikołaja Kopernika.

Kurnatowski, S. 1963. Uwagi o kształtowaniu się stref zasiedlenia dorzecza Obry w czasie od środkowego okresu epoki brązu do późnego średniowiecza. *Archeologia Polski* 8:2, 181-221.

Kurnatowski, S. 1966. Przemiany techniki uprawy roli w czasach między epoką brązową i wczesnym średniowieczem a rozmieszczenie stref zasiedlenia. *Studia z dziejów osadnictwa wiejskiego* 8, 92-99.

Kurnatowski, S. 1974. O zasadach regionalnych badań osadniczych, *Kwartalnik Historii Kultury Materialnej* 22:3, 544-55.

Maciejewski, K. & Rączkowski, W. 2002. Złoty róg czy sznur? Amatorzy w archeologii lotniczej a służby konserwatorskie. *Wielkopolski Biuletyn Konserwatorski* 1, 137-57.

Nowakowski, J. & Rączkowski, W. 2000. Refutation of the myth: new fortified settlement from Late Bronze Age/Early Iron Age in Wielkopolska region (Poland). *Antiquity* 74 (286), 765-66.

Nowakowski, J., Prinke, A. & Rączkowski, W. 1999. Latać czy nie latać?: zdjęcia lotnicze jako kolejny element standardowej procedury w ochronie stanowisk archeologicznych. In M. Dworaczyk, K. Kowalski, A. Porzeziński, S. Słowiński & E. Wilgocki (eds), *Acta Archaeologica Pomoranica, vol. II: konserwatorskie badania archeologiczne w Polsce i w Niemczech – stan prawny, problematyka, osiągnięcia,* 113-52. Szczecin: Stowarzyszenie Naukowe Archeologów Polskich.

ODZ, 1981. Instrukcja wypełniania Karty Ewidencji Stanowiska Archeologicznego. In M. Konopka (ed.), *Zdjęcie Archeologiczne Polski,* 40-48. Warszawa: Ministerstwo Kultury i Sztuki, Generalny Konserwator Zabytków.

Rączkowski, W. 1997. Theories concerning the archaeology of settlement systems: can the stereotypes be changed? *Latvijas Zinatnu Akademijas Vestis* 51:5/6, 54-8.

Rączkowski, W. 2005a. Tradition in power: vicious circle(s) of aerial survey in Poland. In K. Brophy & D. Cowley (eds), *From the air: understanding aerial archaeology,* 151-67. Stroud: Tempus.

Rączkowski, W. 2005b. To overcome infirmity. Current approaches to aerial archaeology in Poland. In J. Bourgeois & M. Meganck (eds), *Aerial photography and archaeology 2003: a century of information,* 121-35. Ghent: Academia Press.

Sosnowski, W. 1996. Aspekty metody AZP na Ziemi Chełmińskiej. In D. Jaskanis (ed.), *Archeologiczne Zdjęcie Polski – metoda i doświadczenia. Próba oceny,* 97-102. Warszawa: Ministerstwo Kultury i Sztuki.

Tabaczyński, S. 1970. *Neolit środkowoeuropejski: podstawy gospodarcze.* Wrocław: Ossolineum.

Trigger, B. 1989. *A history of archaeological thought.* Cambridge: Cambridge University Press.

Woyda, S. 1981. Archeologiczne zdjęcie terenu – ogólne założenia metody w oparciu o doświadczenia mazowieckie. In M. Konopka (ed.), *Zdjęcie Archeologiczne Polski,* 11-21. Warszawa: Ministerstwo Kultury i Sztuki, Generalny Konserwator Zabytków.

6

Crop mark formation on 'difficult' soils in Romania

I.A. Oltean and W.S. Hanson

INTRODUCTION

The intention of this paper is to examine the impact of 'difficult' geological and soil backgrounds on the formation of crop marks in two different areas of Romania: western Transylvania and southern Dobrogea. Within the context of this paper, 'difficult' backgrounds are those where either the soil and/or the subsoil has a tendency to hold water or impede drainage and which, therefore, are not conducive to the formation of crop marks.

The authors have been undertaking aerial reconnaissance in western Transylvania since the summer of 1998, funded in the first instance by the Leverhulme Trust and subsequently by the British Academy, with the aim of increasing understanding of the history and development of the landscape, mainly in the later prehistoric and Roman periods (Hanson and Oltean 2001). The area was chosen not because of any anticipated propensity to reveal crop marks, but because of its coherence as a core region of settlement and communications across a lengthy time span. The Mures Valley is the main communication route between Transylvania and the Pannonian Plain, while the Strei River offers a convenient connection with the plain of Hateg to the south. This in turn provides a nodal point connected to the plains to the south of the Carpathians and to Banat to the west through the famous Iron Gate of Transylvania.

Reconnaissance was aimed at recovering archaeological features visible as crop marks, primarily in cereal crops, since this methodology had never before been applied in Romania. Accordingly, in order to allow for variations in the development of different crops, flying took place in two separate phases each summer, the first in early June and the second in early July. Over the six summers of the project, from 1998-2000 and 2002-

2004, a total of 165 hours of reconnaissance were undertaken. Results varied according to the weather and crop conditions each year, but overall the project proved particularly successful at recording negative crop marks or parchmarks. These indicate the presence of stone structures buried immediately below the present surface which had the effect of reducing access to moisture and nutrients for the growing plants. However, success in identifying examples of positive crop marks of, for example, ditches or pits was much more limited (e.g. Hanson and Oltean 2003; Hanson 2005, 77-83).

More recently attention has turned to a new area in southern Dobrogea between the Danube and the Black Sea immediately to the north of the Bulgarian border, with funding once more provided by the British Academy. The aim of this second project is to evaluate the nature and impact of Roman conquest and colonisation on the transformation of native settlement patterns. These are contextualised within a wider chronological and geographical framework through a comparative analysis of a representative sample of in-site and territory-wide patterns within past landscapes in modern Romania with differing experience of Roman contact. Within this project primary aerial reconnaissance is a more limited strand of data acquisition, with greater emphasis placed on examining available satellite imagery and historical vertical photographs. So far, therefore, only one short season of reconnaissance, aimed at recovering both crop marks and soil marks, has been undertaken in June 2005, though a second is planned for June 2006.

GEOGRAPHICAL, GEOLOGICAL, PEDOLOGICAL AND CLIMATIC BACKGROUND

The geographical focus of the first study area is the western side of Transylvania, which includes the mid-Mures valley, the whole Strei river valley and the Hateg depression to the south. The area is surrounded by higher ground rising gradually on both sides of the valleys as terraced sides of the Carpathian Hills to the west and south, and the Transylvanian tableland to the east. The various mountain ranges extend from altitudes of over 2000m down to 400-600m, while in some places the Transylvanian tableland itself reaches as much as 600-700m in height (Gheorghiu 2001, 2-3; Morariu *et al.* 1966, 25 and 32). This gives an amphitheatre-like appearance to the whole area centred along the main river valleys (27).

The general topography is of hills with smooth slopes and medium fragmentation, grouped around river terraces and valleys. The general appearance of the valleys is that of corridors of varying width. The Mures is a very active river and its alluvial deposits have created a large fertile valley up to 8km wide in places. Its main tributaries, including the Strei, contribute considerably to the general water outflow and to the total quantity of alluvium, resulting in the plain of the Mures being generally wider at its confluences. The tributaries are also responsible for the main changes of direction in the course of the river and the creation of multiple meanders. The Hateg depression to the south is a piedmont plain with fan-shaped terraces of alluvial deposition and a density of small watercourses.

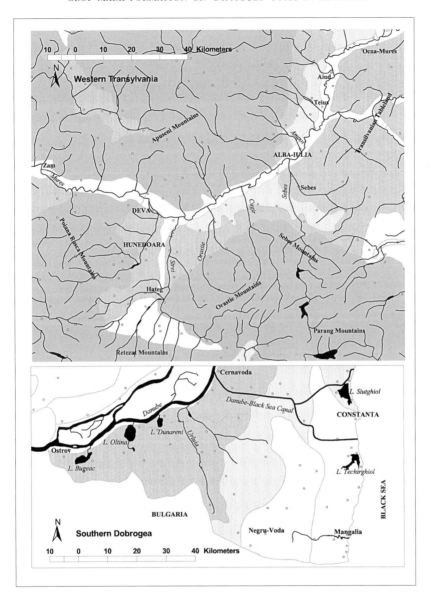

27 The topography of western Transylvania and southern Dobrogea. © *I.A. Oltean*

The geological background of the hills and terraces is represented by clays, marls and sand, with limestone and volcanic intrusions. The soils of the hill and tableland regions are composed mainly of varieties of brown forest soils, affected by podsolisation to various degrees, and of levigated chernozem (Gherasimov *et al.* 1960, 228-31). The cover in the river valleys is composed of alluvial soils, alluvial proto-soils and chernozem. The meadowlands along the rivers are regarded as under regular threat of flooding (Gheorghiu 2001, 5), as was observed by the authors in 1998. Overall there is considerable variation across the region in both geology and soil types.

The climate of the region is usually defined as of temperate-continental type with two moderate seasons, one cold and one hot season each year. The mountains that surround Transylvania behave like a barrier to the more extreme climatic phenomena and ensure a fairly constant microclimate. They stop both the cool, damp masses of air from the west and the cold and violent winds from the east (Morariu *et al.* 1966, 39). Nonetheless, the variation in temperature values during the year is significant. During the winter there are some 100-150 days with temperatures below freezing, occasionally dropping as low as -30° Celsius, while rising to as high as +40° Celsius in the summer. Transylvania and the Carpathian Mountains experience the highest levels of precipitation in Romania, with an average of 1310mm of rain and snow fall each year in the mountains, though average figures for the tableland are 600-700mm. The highest annual rainfall values are generally recorded in June (85-110mm), while the lowest are in February (below 35mm). Nonetheless, periods of drought are not infrequent (Gherasimov *et al.* 1960, 304-6), but rarely last for more than 50 days. There are also local particularities that define microclimatic zones. The Hateg depression, for example, behaves in climatic terms like a mountain depression, which could have up to seven cold months, and the relative humidity is higher than on the lower Strei and Mures valleys (Grumazescu 1975, 119).

The modern landscape of Transylvania is extensively exploited. Indeed, one of its most striking characteristics is the way that cultivation in the past has extended up steeply terraced hillsides to the flat tops of the lower mountain ranges, giving the impression that no suitable cultivable land was ignored. The topographic and climatic particularities of the river valleys with their fertile alluvial soils allow arable cultivation not only on the lower terraces, but also on the large, flat or slightly sloped higher terraces. The steeper slopes with good sun exposure are occupied by orchards or vineyards (Floca 1957, 46). The rest of the land is given over to pasture and forest.

The second study area, southern Dobrogea, is demarcated by the Danube to the west, the Bulgarian border to the south, the Black Sea coast to the east and the Carasu Valley, now the line of the Danube-Black Sea canal, to the north. It is a region of tableland superficially dissected by a limited number of seasonal or dry watercourses into large, mainly flat blocks of land. Heights do not exceed 100-200m with quite abrupt margins facing both the Danube to the west and the Black Sea to the east. The higher land concentrates in the west, sloping gently east and north-east towards the sea and the Carasu Valley, a dip where two tectonic plates meet (27).

The area can conveniently be split into three main geographical regions. In the west along the Danube the tableland is generally defined as a high tableland, with altitudes between 150-200m. The lower, relatively narrow zone directly bordering the Danube is deeply fragmented by large lakes, such as Bugeac and Oltina, which represent silted up fluvial gulfs. The largest region is the maritime tableland, which includes most of the central zone and extends along the coast from lake Tasaul, north of Constanta, to the Bulgarian border. The average altitude is 100m, with a wide coastal terrace 20-40m in height. The mouths of the river valleys are estuarine in origin, but have silted up to form salt-water lakes, such as Techirghiol and Mangalia. Finally, the tableland to the south, around Negru-Voda, has an altitude of 150-170m with a good deal of local variation in relief. It is an area of limestone geology with no riverine exit to the sea and, as a result, exhibits considerable carstic activity, with frequent underground watercourses and cave systems (Gherasimov *et al.* 1960, 249 and 433). Because riverine action across most of the area is so limited, neither erosion nor alluvial deposition has made any substantial impact on the landscape except in the west where there is some deposition by the Danube, particularly in spring when it floods.

The upper geological stratum consists predominantly of a large, flat carapace made up of a thick layer of compacted loess, with limestone in the south, occasionally mixed with marls and clays. Other than that, there is very little variation across the region. The soil too shows limited variation, consisting of different types of chernozem, mainly light in texture. In a few places, however, particularly in the east along the coast, there are small areas of much heavier chernozem.

Dobrogea is Romania's warmest and driest region, with some 450mm of annual precipitation, much of it in the spring. The highest annual rainfall values are recorded in June (40-50mm), with the lowest in February (40-45mm). However, the superficial impression of consistency is a false one, as rainfall tends to be intense and short-lived. The climate is continental arid, with the exception of the maritime zone. Temperatures range from on or just below freezing in January and February to +30° Celsius in mid-summer, with milder weather beginning in April and ending in November. The area is susceptible to hot dry winds emanating form the Russian Steppe in the summer months. As a result of the geology and climate, water supply is a problem across much of Dobrogea. There are no naturally flowing rivers across the tableland, only 'dry' valleys of seasonal character, fed by snow melt and precipitation in the spring, so that water for cultivation has to be derived entirely from precipitation.

Given the local topography and the nature of the geological and pedological background, it is not surprising that the modern landscape is predominantly given over to arable cultivation. This encompasses the whole of the maritime tableland, along with a narrow strip of the Danubian tableland around the large fluvial lakes. Pastureland, along with small patches given over to forest, is located mainly in the higher and more fragmented Danubian tableland and to a more limited extent in the southernmost area, where the water shortage restricts cultivation. The arable cultivation is focused mostly on cereals, but several slopes, particularly along the Carasu Valley around Medgidia, are occupied by vineyards producing some of the finest wines in Romania.

CROP MARK DISTRIBUTION IN RELATION TO SOIL TYPES AND GEOLOGICAL BACKGROUND

It is clear from the brief descriptions above that the environmental conditions for aerial archaeological research in the two study areas are very different. The sites photographed were located on as many as 14 types of soil and up to 36 different geological compositions, all with very variable physical and chemical structures. In respect of both its soils and geology, southern Dobrogea was the most uniform in nature (with only four

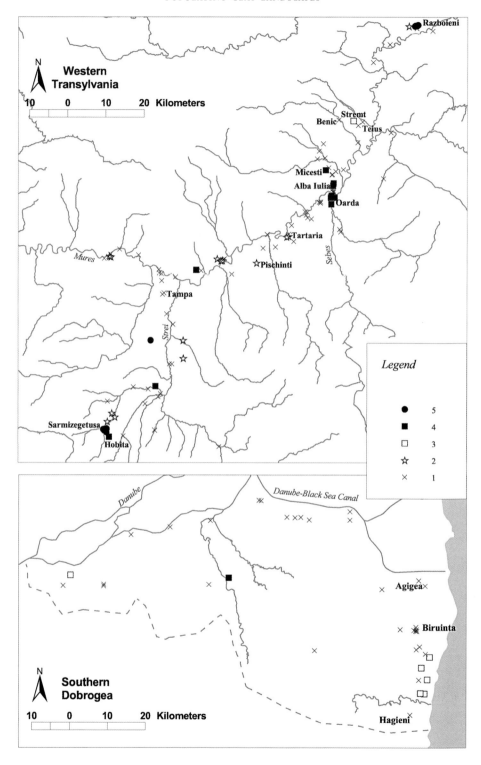

28 Geological conditions for crop mark sites in western Transylvania and southern Dobrogea according to moisture retention capacity (1–lowest; 5–highest). © *I.A. Oltean*

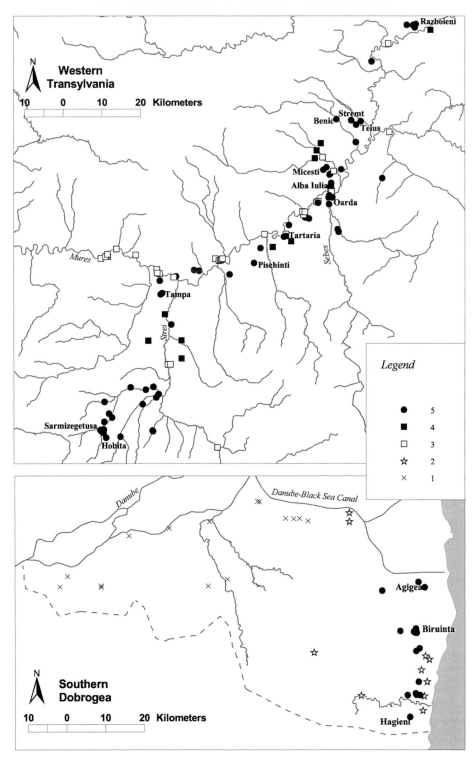

29 Soil conditions for crop mark sites in western Transylvania and southern Dobrogea according to moisture retention capacity (1-lowest; 5-highest). © I.A. Oltean

different soil types and six geological variants), while western Transylvania was the most fragmented (with 10 soil types and 30 geological variants). Despite this variety, however, it was possible to group both soils and geological variants each into five broad categories, ranked according to their water retention properties. The distribution of crop marks was then considered against the background of these groupings, within the constraints of the resolution of the available geological maps.

In western Transylvania, as would be expected, the recovery of crop mark sites has been primarily successful on sand and gravel subsoils (*28*). Of the 108 crop mark sites recorded in the study area in western Transylvania, some 69 were in areas where the substratum was alluvial sands and gravels while the remaining 39 sites were located on heavier, less well-drained subsoils, which include clays and/or marls in their composition. Marls have similar properties to clays in terms of impeding the filtering down of surface precipitation to the water table and both have, therefore, been included within the category of most difficult geological backgrounds. In Dobrogea, out of 42 crop mark sites recorded so far, as many as 30 are located on loess deposits (*28*). Given that the loess is essentially dust deposited by the wind action, its subsequent compaction might be expected to give it similarly poor drainage properties. However, because it tends to preserve numerous vertical mini-channels created over time by the penetration of fine roots, it drains both quickly and well and has been categorised accordingly.

Again quite a high proportion (34) of the crop mark sites from western Transylvania are on floodplain and delta soils with mixed alluvium and sands, only four are on brown forest soils less affected by podsolisation, but some 64 sites were recorded on very wet soils, mainly levigated chernozem and heavily podsolised brown forest soil (*29*). Several of the soils in the study areas have a tendency to retain water, including rendzinas, mountain soils, and specific types of both chernozem and forest soil. In western Transylvania the rendzinas (fertile lime-rich soils with a dark, friable, humus-rich surface layer) cover marls and clays whose poor drainage properties are transferred to that topsoil cover. Also occurring only in western Transylvania, the mountain soils are to be found predominantly at higher altitudes where land use tends to be alpine pasture or high forests. Accordingly, crop mark recovery on both these types of soils was extremely poor and archaeological sites tend to be recorded only if extant. The less fertile brown forest soils found in western Transylvania at altitudes from 125–150m to 800m or even 1000m have a variable degree of moisture retention. Those affected by degradation (podsolisation) tend to be very wet and with low aeration, so that man-made drainage is recommended for their use in agriculture. The water from precipitation affects the mineral content of these soils which is degraded and washed down the profile where it accumulates as clay and impedes drainage (Gherasimov *et al.* 1960, 496, fig. 197). Interestingly, only four sites identified on the basis of crop mark evidence (e.g. Batiz, Chitid) were located on these weakly and medium podsolised soils. However, these soils are of more limited distribution and of more recent conversion to arable, so a higher proportion (9) of the sites identified are extant. There was a far higher occurrence of crop mark recovery (22) in the heavily podsolised areas in the Hateg depression, predominantly above sands and gravels, but also on heavier geology in the west, as for example at Sarmizegetusa and Hobita.

Chernozem is a fertile soil, rich in humus, which is characteristic of natural grassland in cool to temperate semi-arid climates. The types of chernozem predominant in southern Dobrogea are light in texture and colour and offer great conditions for crop mark formation (3). However, the levigated (finely powdered) chernozem is a heavy soil. As in the podsolisation of forest soils, the mineral content in its structure is degraded by the water which transforms it into clay particles and transports it deeper into the soil profile. This fertile and compact stratum can be as thick as 134cm, below which it becomes sandier in texture. Because of its high humus and reasonable water content, it is intensively used for cereal cultivation. It is present in limited areas in southern Dobrogea overlying loess along the sea coast, particularly around lake Techirghiol (where 17 crop mark sites have been identified), and more extensively in western Transylvania above marl and/or clay deposits (with 38 crop mark sites).

CASE STUDIES

Looking at the specific site data in more detail, a number of patterns of occurrence become apparent. Firstly, a surprising number of sites were recorded on heavy soils overlying poorly draining subsoil. These occur mainly in areas where clays, marls and marl-clays are present in the deeper geology, layered with sands and gravels, but also with limestones, conglomerates or volcanic rock. The heavy soils in these cases are podsolised forest soils or levigated chernozem. Several sites have been recorded around the town of Sarmizegetusa, for example, all as negative crop marks in a cereal crop or parchmarks in rough pasture in an area of podsolised forest soils: on the Delinestilor Hill at Hobita, to the east of the town of Sarmizegetusa, were traces of a rectangular building, probably a Roman villa; immediately outside the town on its south-east side a small isolated square stone building, probably a mausoleum, was noted; and to the NW of the town were slight traces of buildings, possibly another external villa.

At Oarda, which lies on raised ground by a small stream overlooking the river Sebes approximately 4km south-west of Alba, the subsoil consists of a mixture of conglomerates, sandstones and marl-clays and the soil is a levigated chernozem. Nonetheless, quite extensive remains of Roman villa buildings were recorded as negative crop marks in the dry summer of 2000, spreading across an area *c.*100m x 120m. A site visit indicated that the field was littered with Roman building materials, suggesting that the remains were quite near to the surface. In very similar geological and soil conditions at least two adjacent rectangular buildings on the same alignment, again probably a Roman villa (*30*), were identified between Micesti and the historic town of Alba Iulia, while on the southern edge of the town a series of closely spaced properties, demarcated by stone walls, containing irregular rectangular buildings and occasional pits have been recorded, representing part of the Roman *municipium* outside the legionary fortress.

Finally at Razboieni, in an area of sands, marl-clays and gravel, a range of negative crop marks have been recorded over several seasons. These include a series of rectangular stone buildings along a network of roads to the west and south of the fort, representing the associated civil settlement extending for at least 1km (Oltean and Hanson 2001), as well as

30 Negative crop marks outline the foundations of a possible Roman villa at Micesti in early July 2004. © *W.S. Hanson*

the road layout and some of the internal buildings of the large Roman fort itself. Interestingly, however, no trace is visible of the ditches which would have surrounded the fort.

Only a small number of sites (six in total) have been recorded on heavy soils overlying medium draining subsoils, that is on levigated chernozem overlying a variety of geological deposits in which sands and gravels are predominant, but marls and marl-clays, along with limestones and sandstones, are present in smaller quantities. Both negative and positive crop marks have been recorded, including two ditched enclosures at Tartaria and two examples of isolated rectangular stone buildings, possibly later medieval or relatively modern, at Stremt and Pischinti. However, since none of the sites has been investigated on the ground, it is possible that the occurrence of crop marks on these sites may have coincided with localised areas of better draining subsoil.

However, several examples of positive crop marks are apparent in Transylvania on a combination of heavy soils and reasonably well-drained subsoil. For example, a cluster of very regular rectangular sunken houses revealed at the south-eastern end of the modern village of Berghin represents a multi-period (Dacian-Roman) settlement (*31*). The site is located on sands and gravels, while the topsoil is a pseudo-rendzina (a dark soil, heavy and rich in humus which behaves like a rendzina). Similarly, a series of large sub-circular pits, probably bomb craters, and a possible prehistoric enclosure were revealed at Tampa; also a scatter of small pits was apparent at Teius (*32*), their identification as funerary or ritual pits and their Bronze Age date confirmed by excavation (information from Dr M. Grigor). Both sites are located on alluvial gravels and sands overlain by levigated chernozem.

31 Rectangular light-toned (reversal) positive crop marks indicate sunken houses and pits of a possible Daco-Roman settlement at Berghin, early July 2004. © *W.S. Hanson*

32 Positive crop marks of small Bronze Age pits in an area under archaeological investigation prior to building development at Teius, early July 2004. © *W.S. Hanson*

33 Extant tumuli and, to the left, positive crop marks of the surrounding ditch and mound of a tumulus adjacent to a possible rectangular ditched enclosure at Biruinta, early June 2005.
© I.A. Oltean and W.S. Hanson

Further examples benefiting from similar conditions were also recorded in southern Dobrogea, which demonstrates that the crop mark formation in difficult soil conditions in Romania is not a phenomenon restricted to western Transylvania. In all cases the sites were located on heavy, levigated chernozem, overlying well-draining loess. At Biruinta a range of features was apparent. These included a large group of tumuli, some of which were extant. Their surrounding ditches and in one case slight traces of the internal mound showed as positive crop marks, along with an adjacent rectangular ditched enclosure which was possibly funerary in character (*33*). Nearby were a number of pits, both small examples which were possibly burials and larger ones, possibly sunken houses, all showing as positive crop marks. Similarly, in two adjacent tumuli at Agigea the remains of both the mound and, in one case, its surrounding ditch, showed as positive crop marks.

Negative crop marks of buildings are also well-attested on this soil and subsoil combination in both areas. In Transylvania, at Benic, an apparently isolated small square stone building was recorded adjacent to the river Galda, in a location where the county gazetteer mentions the discovery in 1935 of a Roman altar dedicated to Jupiter (Moga and Ciugudean 1995, 53-4), while at Batiz a cluster of large rectangular stone buildings, probably a Roman village, extended across an area of at least 1ha (*34*). An even larger, probably Roman, settlement was identified in Dobrogea at Hagieni (*35*) where a series of square and rectangular stone buildings on the same alignment extended across an area of more than 8ha.

34 Negative crop marks showing stone building foundations of a probable Roman settlement within the modern village of Batiz, early July 2004. © *W.S. Hanson*

35 Large settlement at Hagieni visible as negative crop marks of building foundations in early June 2005. © *I.A. Oltean and W.S. Hanson*

36 Combination of positive crop marks indicating the pits and sunken houses of Bronze Age, Dacian and Daco-Roman settlements and negative crop marks of stone building foundations of a Roman villa at Vintu de Jos, early July 2000. © *W.S. Hanson*

CONCLUSION

Initial work in western Transylvania led the authors to confront the issue of the impact of heavy soils on crop mark formation, as well as to consider the character of the archaeological features that are more likely to produce crop marks. This requirement was reinforced by the contrasting results obtained from preliminary work in the very different environmental conditions pertaining in southern Dobrogea.

The preponderance of negative crop marks and general dearth of positive crop marks was a characteristic of the survey area in Transylvania which rapidly became apparent. That this was in some way related to the characteristics of the local geology and soils, particularly the preponderance of alluvium was proposed (Hanson and Oltean 2003). More detailed analysis above, however, suggests that that is an over-simplification. On denser, non-alluvial subsoils, only four sites (Razboieni, Alba Iulia and two at Tartaria) have produced positive rather than negative crop marks, though even at Razboieni the site of the Roman fort was defined by its roads and internal buildings, not its surrounding ditches. Positive crop marks are largely confined to well-draining subsoils. Where sites have been recorded on heavier subsoils, they are almost exclusively in the form of negative crop marks. This is perhaps best exemplified at Vintu de Jos, where rectangular buildings of a Roman villa, its identification confirmed by the discovery of *tegulae* on the surface of the field during subsequent fieldwalking, were located on the first terrace of the Mures River adjacent to traces of pits and sunken houses of a Dacian village, both of which were visible at the same time (*36*). The soil is a damp, undeveloped chernozem, but the negative crop marks which revealed the existence of the villa were located in an area of heavier clay subsoil, the positive crop marks of the Dacian settlement on sand. Where more detailed work has been done on sites revealed as negative crop marks, as at Vintu de Jos, Oarda and Cigmau, it is also clear that the soils are relatively shallow with the archaeological remains lying relatively close to the modern surface.

The recovery of crop marks in areas of reasonably well-draining subsoils, such as sands, gravels and loess, is perhaps unsurprising, even when the topsoil cover is relatively heavy and water-retentive. What is more surprising is the number of sites recorded on heavy soils, such as podsolised forest soils or levigated chernozem, overlying poorly draining subsoils, such as clays and marls. The potential for the recovery of negative crop marks in similar geological areas is clearly worthy of investigation in other European regions.

BIBLIOGRAPHY

Floca, O. 1957. *Regiunea Hunedoara. Ghid turistic.* Deva.
Gherasimov I.P. *et al.* 1960. *Monografia geografica a republicii populare Romine.* Vol. I-II. Bucharest: Editura Academiei Republicii Populare Romine.
Gheorghiu, G.L. 2001. *Asezari si fortificatii dacice in zona cursului mijlociu al Muresului sec.II i.e.n-I e.n.* Unpublished PhD thesis, Babes-Bolyai University, Cluj-Napoca.
Grumazescu, C. 1975. *Depresiunea Hategului. Studiu geomorphologic.* Bucharest.
Hanson, W.S. 2005. Sun, sand and see: creating bias in the archaeological record. In K. Brophy & D. Cowley (eds), *From the air: understanding aerial archaeology,* 73-85. Stroud: Tempus.
Hanson, W.S. & Oltean, I.A. 2001. Recent aerial survey in Western Transylvania: problems and potential. In R.H. Bewley & W. Rączkowski (eds), *Aerial archaeology – developing future practice,* 109-115 and 353-55. Amsterdam: Nato Science Series.
Hanson, W.S. & Oltean, I.A. 2003. The identification of Roman buildings from the air: recent discoveries in Western Transylvania. *Archaeological Prospection* 10, 101-17.
Moga, V. & Ciugudean, H. 1995. *Repertoriul arheologic al judetului Alba.* Alba Iulia: Bibliotheca Musei Apulensis II.
Morariu, T., Cucu, V. & Velcea, I. 1966. *The geography of Romania.* Bucharest.
Oltean, I.A. & Hanson, W.S. 2001. Military *vici* in Roman Dacia: an aerial perspective. *Acta Musei Napocensis* 38:1, 123-34.

7

Seventy-five years *v.* ninety minutes: implications of the 1996 Bedfordshire vertical aerial survey on our perceptions of clayland archaeology

Rog Palmer

INTRODUCTION

Examination of an archaeologically rich aerial photographic survey of Bedfordshire prompted a comparison of different methods of aerial observation and recording that are used to gather archaeological data. That comparison leads to the suggestion of reasons for the absence of archaeological information on clay soils among the aerial photographs taken by our specialist observers. A small area of clayland has been mapped to show examples of its archaeological features and the paper concludes with comments about the implications of the pedologically biased distribution for archaeology and suggests how future aerial survey may endeavour to counteract this.

Archaeological prospection is assisted by three types of 'remote sensing' which produce aerial photographs or images of the ground on which may be recorded traces left by past communities. An observer, sometimes an archaeologist but not always so, can fly in a light aircraft to visually examine the ground and take photographs of anything that is of interest. Photographs taken in this way will be 'observer-directed' or 'observer-targeted' and are usually oblique views (i.e. at a slanting angle to the ground) of a single site taken using a hand-held camera. This type of activity had its origins between the two world wars when it was honed to a fine art by Major G.W.G. Allen who photographed archaeological features in the Thames Valley and other areas of southern England (Allen 1984). Such flying can attempt to be systematic so as to fully observe an area of land or can meander about to examine land that is thought likely to give good results while ignoring that in between. Such observer-directed activity is the main kind of archaeological aerial survey carried out in many countries at the present time. The main advantages claimed for this means of survey are its relative low cost, its ability to take advantage of local weather conditions, its production of high-definition photographs that are capable of recording considerable detail and, if the lighting is appropriate, it can illustrate clearly the context of a site. A main disadvantage is that an observer has to see (and understand) a feature before it can be photographed. Biases in this method of survey were reviewed recently by a number of contributors in *From the Air* (Brophy and Cowley 2005).

A second method of recording the ground from above is by vertical aerial survey which is usually, but not necessarily, carried out using a twin-engine aircraft within which is mounted a large and expensive camera. The camera points straight down at the ground (hence the term 'vertical') and its exposures can be timed to produce a series of overlapping photographs along a flight-line or series of sideways-overlapping lines that will totally record an area of the ground. The photographs can be examined stereoscopically to recreate a three-dimensional image of the ground surface or, in digital form, can be joined seamlessly to create a mosaic for use within a Geographical Information System. The first archaeological aerial survey in Britain was undertaken to produce vertical photographs of (mainly) upstanding sites that were already known (Crawford and Keiller 1928). Since that date there has been minimal archaeological use of this means of aerial photography although millions of vertical photographs have been taken for other purposes. Advantages include the fact that an area survey will record *all* the ground below the camera including any archaeological features that may be visible at the time and that the photographs are taken for serious (i.e. stereoscopic) examination of the ground. Main disadvantages are seen as the high cost and, since no archaeological organisation owns a suitable aircraft and camera, the delay that may occur between commissioning and taking the photographs (see Coleman; this volume). The latter means that there is a chance of missing the short 'season' in which, for example, crop-marked archaeological information is visible.

A third means of acquiring an aerial view is to use photographs or images taken from satellites. Archaeologists are increasingly using these, especially in countries where maps or conventional aerial photographs are not available, and the best image resolution from commercial satellites is as good or better than that of 1:12,000 scale vertical photographs. The cost of images is high but the existing QuickBird satellite has a revisit rate of three days and its successor, WorldView which was due to be launched in 2006, is able to overfly the same spot every 24 hours. If necessary, either satellite can be activated in a short time to collect images of a specified area and so provides a rapidly responsive means of 'aerial photography' that can be used to take advantage of, for example, crop conditions and forecast clear skies. Stereoscopic pairs or runs can be taken to aid interpretation (Digital Globe 2006).

BEDFORDSHIRE'S 1996 VERTICAL AERIAL SURVEY

Vertical photographs are commissioned by many local government authorities on a regular basis, often at five- or ten-year intervals. They provide an up-to-date overview of the county or district and serve a range of purposes, archaeology being one, within various local authority departments. These photographs are normally taken at 1:10,000 scale and as overlapping frames that can be viewed stereoscopically.

Stephen Coleman is the Historic Environment Information Officer for Bedfordshire County Council and is one of the people who decides when new vertical aerial surveys of the county are to be taken (see Coleman; this volume). It was due to his involvement in the planning stages that full stereoscopic 1:10,000 scale vertical aerial photographs of the whole of Bedfordshire were taken in mid-July 1996. It was hoped that this would be an appropriate date to record a sample of crop-marked information (Coleman; this volume). The summer date and the fact that 1996 was an extremely dry summer resulted in a superb archaeologically informative set of photographs which show what may be possible to attain anywhere in the country for reasonable expenditure (Mills 2003; 2005; Palmer 2005).

I was lucky enough to see the 1996 photographs a few days after they had been received by Bedfordshire County Council where I was examining the most recent aerial photographs as part of an English Heritage-funded project to identify surviving medieval fields (Hall 2001). Even after working with aerial photographs for 30 years I was amazed by the quantity of crop-marked archaeological features that was visible. The photographs showed that most cereals on gravel (and other well-drained soils) were almost fully ripe, with some fields already harvested. However, the growth of crops on clay lagged behind those on lighter soils and most were various shades of green. On clay, a prolific number of crop-marked archaeological features could be seen in fields of cereals and grass. Thus this set of vertical aerial photographs recorded, perhaps for the first time, a dense distribution of buried archaeological sites, many of which were previously unknown, on soils usually regarded as unproductive or 'difficult'. To find out more about this new material, at the end of my medieval task I made time to examine three north–south flight-lines of photographs that spanned the Great Ouse Valley and extended into Cambridgeshire. The flying time to produce these three lines of photographs was in the region of 90 minutes. From these photographs, the locations of features and their approximate extents were sketched on a 1:50,000 map within an area of 300sq km. When this rapid scan was completed, my map showed just over 300 sites, most of which were on clay soils and most of which were previously unknown (37). Such a dense distribution of archaeological sites raised the question of why so much of it was new. The Great Ouse Valley and its environs had been examined many times in the history of archaeological aerial reconnaissance and the work of Chris Cox who flew over the area in the early 1990s proved that sites on clay were visible in other than drought years.

COMPARISON OF 75 YEARS AND 90 MINUTES

The next need was to compare this new distribution with one of sites recorded on observer-directed photographs that had been taken during archaeological aerial survey.

Sources for that information were Cambridge University (CUCAP, who were, in effect, the local fliers for this area) and the Royal Commission on the Historical Monuments of England (RCHME – now absorbed into English Heritage). At the time this distribution map was prepared the location of archaeological sites photographed by CUCAP was obtained using their National Grid Reference card index. This had been extracted from their main catalogue and included only those photographs that recorded archaeological features. RCHME provided a list of photographs in National Grid order which, because they had no subject index, were all assumed to record archaeological features.

Archaeological flights by what was to become CUCAP were begun by Kenneth St Joseph using RAF aircraft in 1945. Initially the hours flown per year were few but the results obtained and the interest generated led to the purchase of their own aircraft in 1960 and a continuing increase in flying time (Wilson 1995, 420-21). A considerable part of this flying time was dedicated to archaeological survey. St Joseph's retirement in 1980 and changes in University policy meant that CUCAP had to earn its keep and consequently less archaeological photography could be done and had virtually ceased by 1990. Thus, for the purpose of this comparative exercise, the list of sites from CUCAP had the potential to cover the 45 years between 1945 and 1989.

The Air Photographs Unit of the RCHME was established late in 1966 and began its first archaeological survey flights in 1967 (Hampton 1989, 17-18). Their collection includes photographs taken by themselves and others and is now part of English Heritage's National Monuments Record (NMR). This collection was searched for photographs taken before the end of 1996 to provide data for the observer-directed distribution map, so adding a further 30 years of flying time to that undertaken for archaeological survey.

A first concern was to establish whether a good sample of sites on the claylands had been obtained during those 75 years of archaeological observation. A distribution map was prepared to show the location of photographed sites on a background of soils. It also distinguished photographs taken to the end of 1989 from those taken between 1990 and 1996 in case a difference in reconnaissance practice could be identified that showed, for example, an increase in observation over the clay areas. The completed distribution map shows a predominance of aerial photography on the gravels and other 'easier' soils (38) with the few pre-1990 sites recorded on clays being mostly winter photographs of upstanding remains. The post-1990 record on clay is largely due to the work of Chris Cox who received an annual grant from RCHME to examine the Cambridgeshire clays between the Great Ouse Valley and Bourn airfield, some 6km east of the mapped area. Comparison of figures 37 and 38 shows two almost mutually exclusive distributions, one resulting from archaeological research, the other recorded by chance. It had then to be asked why these distributions are so different.

WHY THE DIFFERENCE?

A lot of the absence of earlier evidence is likely to be due to the accepted 'fact' that clay soils were not settled before medieval times or, if they had been, they would not show

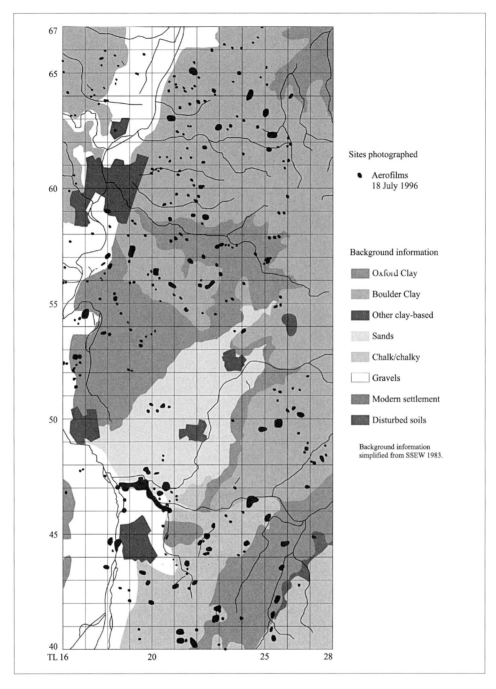

Sites photographed

• Aerofilms
  18 July 1996

Background information

▨ Oxford Clay

▨ Boulder Clay

■ Other clay-based

▨ Sands

▨ Chalk/chalky

☐ Gravels

▨ Modern settlement

▨ Disturbed soils

Background information
simplified from SSEW 1983.

37 More than 300 archaeological sites were identified in parts of Bedfordshire and Cambridgeshire during rapid examination of vertical photographs taken by Simmons Aerofilms on 18 July 1996. The map shows the sketched extent of the features and their location on a simplified soil map. The Great Ouse River runs up the west side of the map and the modern settlements include Biggleswade (TL1945) and St Neots (TL1860). Most of the sites on clay soils had not been known before this photography. See figure *38. Copyright: Rog Palmer. Background based on SSEW 1983 © Crown Copyright. Licence number 100028850*

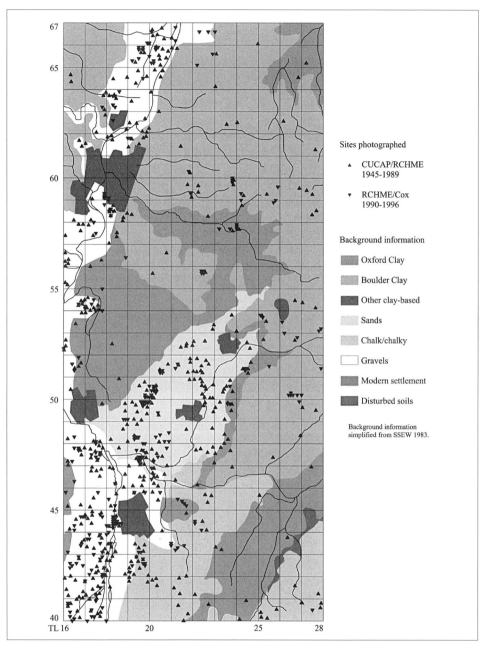

Sites photographed

▲ CUCAP/RCHME
1945-1989

▼ RCHME/Cox
1990-1996

Background information

Oxford Clay

Boulder Clay

Other clay-based

Sands

Chalk/chalky

Gravels

Modern settlement

Disturbed soils

Background information
simplified from SSEW 1983.

38 The same area as figure *37* showing the distribution of archaeological targets photographed by observers between 1945 and 1996 with different symbols to indicate those taken before and after 1990 (see text). The location of sites shows the six-figure grid references, within 100m, listed in the indexes of CUCAP and NMRC. The majority of photographed sites are on the well-drained soils, the river gravels and sands, a survey practice that seems to have remained unchanged before and after 1990. Most of the sites photographed on clay before 1990 were upstanding earthworks, but between 1992 and 1994 the distribution on clay was enhanced by the work of Chris Cox. This map includes nine sites photographed by RCHME during flights across the area on 16 and 24 July 1996. Three of those are on clay. *Copyright: Rog Palmer. Background based on SSEW 1983 © Crown Copyright. Licence number 100028850*

39 This slightly enhanced photograph illustrates the usual poor contrast of crop-marked ditches on clay soil. Features such as these tend to affect growth late in the summer, although the cereal is still light green in colour with darker crops above the buried ditches. Other crops in the area have already been harvested, making it likely that this field was planted with spring-sown wheat.
© *Rog Palmer: 95.139/06, 21 July 1995*

ditched features through differences in crop growth. Some airborne observers did look for sites on 'difficult' soils, but in a desultory way, preferring the relative riches and easier hunting on adjacent gravels (Wilson 1978, 49). Another reason that may explain why sites on clay remained unseen could be to do with what aerial photographers call the 'crop mark season' – the few weeks each year when variations in ripening crops may indicate sub-surface differences (see below). Observers may base this 'season' on changes they see in cereals on the lighter soils that they more frequently over-fly and assume that crops on all soils are behaving similarly. However, cereals on clay soils tend to ripen some two weeks later than those on lighter soils. Furthermore, Chris Cox's unpublished observations showed that if sites on clay are going to become visible in crops it will be late in the growing season; in normal years perhaps a week or so before they are harvested (*39*). By this time many other observers may have thought their 'season' was over and have ended their summer flying.

It may be helpful to explain briefly what happens to crops in a 'normal' summer (see also Evans; this volume). The essential theory is that soil-filled holes in the ground create a larger reservoir for moisture and other nutrients above which crops initially grow more lushly and faster than those plants in shallower soil. This produces what aerial photographers refer to as a 'green-on-green' difference (*40*). Later, as the crop ripens, plants over deeper soil remain green for longer and are visible against a yellow background (*41*). In some crops, just before harvest, the green crops 'reverse' and change to become a very light colour against what is often, by then, a dusty-brown coloured background (*42*). In Britain these crop changes take place earlier in the warmer south than they do in the north.

The lateness of these colour changes in cereal crops over clay may help explain the absence of sites on clay in the CUCAP photographs as the flying logs show the annual pilgrimages to the north, and ultimately to Roman Scotland, tended to follow the ripening crop up the country (R. Whimster, pers. comm., while preparing Whimster 1983). Therefore, during the years when St Joseph was almost single-handedly recording the whole of Britain, there would have been no observation over the English claylands at the appropriate time of year.

Absence of RCHME aerial reconnaissance over clay may be expected because their early years of flying tended to concentrate on areas of current and proposed inventories – Dorset, Hampshire, east Cambridgeshire, the Yorkshire Wolds and (in later years)

40 In the original colour photograph, crops in the larger field left of the track are dark green, those to the right are a lighter green with patches that are almost yellow. The darker crop may be wheat, the lighter barley. In both fields, lines and polygons of darker crop can be seen over deeper soil that has filled natural fissures in the limestone bedrock, archaeological ditches and other cut features. This is fairly typical of the ways in which cut features show in crops as they are beginning to ripen.
© *Rog Palmer: 95.96/20, 22 June 1995*

41 The crop here is probably barley but the field has been sown on different dates with the earlier and riper crop in the upper part of the photograph. The lower crop is a mid-green colour with darker green remaining above the deeper soil, in this case including medieval furrows, a small quarry and archaeological ditches and possible pits. The upper field is a deep yellow colour with some green patches (here darker toned) remaining and the same green crops indicate deeper soil. Note that one of the medieval furrows shows as the same tone, or colour, in both areas of this differently ripening cereal. This site is only 7km from that in figure *40* but is on river gravel. Comparison of the two figures suggests that some of the differences that are visible on photographs of the same date are most likely due to dissimilar soils or different dates of planting. © *Rog Palmer: 95.96/17, 22 June 1995*

Northamptonshire. Absence in more recent years cannot be explained as, by the early 1980s, local fliers such as Glenn Foard and Jim Pickering had made concentrated efforts to examine their local clays (Northamptonshire and Leicestershire respectively) and their results clearly demonstrated that sites on clays could be seen and photographed by a persistent observer. What was missing were more of those persistent observers in other parts of the country. Another reason to explain the absence of observation relates to the need to justify expenditure by showing a high number of sites photographed (Featherstone *et al.* 1995). Such a requirement by the paymasters (and indeed by the photographers' egos) would, and did, result in a concentration of observation above soils known to be rewarding. This is unlikely to change in our management-heavy world where success is measured by quantity rather than quality.

A final reason to explain the absence of evidence may relate to interest, understanding and aesthetics. Before taking a photograph, the airborne observer has first to recognise differences in crops, soil colours or topography and then decide whether these are of interest or not. Sites on clay can, in 'normal' years, appear as fragments of information or as poorly contrasting crop-marked sites (see *39*) which do not result in impressive

42 Crops in another field on river gravel are dusty brown and close to their harvesting date. Some of the archaeological and natural features have caused crops above them to turn almost white while above others they remain green. The light tone is what aerial photographers call 'reversal'. It does not occur over every deep feature and, in this illustration, probably indicates that the ditch of the inner rectangle is of different depth or fill content to that of the outer enclosure. © *Rog Palmer: 94.150/13, 14 July 1994*

photographs and poorly visible sites are often poorly photographed. So, if these slight traces are not understood they may not be photographed by an observer. The lure of aesthetics can be identified in the work of many observer-photographers who are likely to take many photographs of a clearly visible site but may take only one where evidence is hazy. This is just the opposite of an aerial photographic interpreter's requirements who needs more photographs of indistinct traces and may use only one of a high-contrast site. These add to the reasons why so few sites on clay were photographed by archaeologist-observers in the present study area between 1946 and 1996 and why this imbalance is known to be country-wide.

TYPES OF SITE

Jessica Mills (2003; 2005) has suggested that differences can be identified in past uses of clay and gravels soils. My quick examination of the 1996 Bedfordshire verticals left me with the initial impression that the clays seemed populated by a predominance of isolated near-circular or curvilinear enclosures that were too big to be Bronze Age round barrows. More detailed examination of the photographs and recent excavation shows these to be only one component of the clay landscape which includes a range of ditched enclosures plus traces of more extensive systems of fields, tracks and other forms of land allotment (43) (see also Deegan and Mills; this volume).

There are varying levels of refinement at which any area, from a few adjacent fields to a county-wide landscape, can be examined and discussed. However, one of the great problems with evidence from aerial photographs is that guess work and probability become the main basis for dating features if no other information is available. Certain characteristics of features, their morphology and their relationships with others, are able sometimes to fix a site within a certain date range although these are more reliable with 'ritual' and military features (e.g. causewayed enclosures, henges, defended camps and forts) than with the sprawl of low-status occupation that covered the greater part of the land. Material collected during fieldwalking can enhance these guesses but there are assumptions and problems concerning the veracity of relationships between material collected from the surface and the buried pits and ditches from which that material may have derived (Palmer 1996, 14). So even with those additional data our analyses and phasing of crop-marked features may be reliant on little more than dubiously informed guesses.

There are, however, certain things that can be *suggested* from examination of mapped air photographic evidence which shows form, association, and from which accurate measurements can be taken. Of these the most reliable comments may concern relationships between features although even here some consideration of dating is necessary, and what follows provides a brief demonstration of this within a small part of Bedfordshire.

Figure 43 covers less than 5sq km, an area that is hardly worth gracing with the word landscape. Yet it is at this local level that associations and relationships can be suggested or identified that may then be extended over a larger area to examine a different level in the organisation of past societies. Bearing in mind that figure 43 is based on photographs of one date only (for comparison see second figure in Mills this volume, which was based on all available photographs) some of the apparent spaces between mapped features could be due to unresponsive crops in 1996 rather than actual absence. Even so, this small area shows six groups of features that could be called 'sites' (A–C, E–G) and may show foci of settlement. Among and between those six sites are observable relationships that can offer some insight into past behaviour. From the evidence of just the 1996 photographs, site A stands in relative isolation although once it clearly extended north and south of its presently recorded limits. So it offers little information beyond the fact that there was a settlement there at some date. Site E is similarly isolated.

Site B could be described as a roughly D-shaped enclosure with internal and external features, one of which shows superimposition. Extending south from one corner of B is a sinuous ditch that turns abruptly to the west at a point where it could have linked with ditches of site C. So these two sites, or parts of them, could have been in use at the same time and been part of one larger system of land division. A short length of a second sinuous ditch can be seen near the south-west corner of site B and it is tempting to suggest that this may have extended to what appears to be a form of funnel entrance feature in the north-eastern bend of D. So a first result of examining these mapped relationships is the suggestion that two sites that may have been contemporary

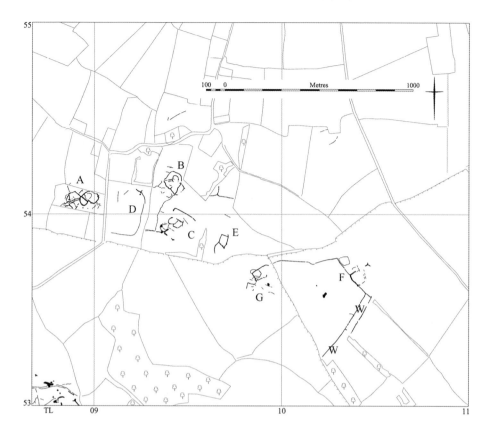

43 A small area of past (black) and modern (grey) landscape in parts of Great Barford, Renhold and Wilden parishes has been mapped from sections of two transformed Bedfordshire 1996 vertical aerial photographs. Ditched features and pits were visible as darker growth in fields of light-green wheat. Barley has ripened to a uniform brown colour and was featureless. The text includes discussion of the features, their relationships to one another and their possible dates.

A selection of natural, recent and modern information was also visible as crop-marked information on the photographs but has not been mapped for this illustration. In 1996 there were no large modern settlements in the area, only isolated farmsteads. So the main areas that would be 'blank' on aerial photographs are the woods and the unresponsive crops. The area is entirely on clay and is to the north-east of Bedford. Soils are predominantly Boulder Clay with a tongue of Oxford Clay along the northern edge which may be the cause of the lack of crop-marked information in that part of the map. Grid intervals are 1km, parish boundaries are dotted lines. © *Rog Palmer*

settlements (B and C) may have been linked to a system of larger enclosures (including D) that may have been associated with stock raising (as can be inferred from the funnel entrance). The repetitive use of 'may have been' in the previous sentence is deliberate and emphasises the degree of guesswork in this analysis. But at present it is the only way in which we can begin to approach any un-enhanced evidence that is interpreted from aerial photographs.

Sites F and G are obviously joined by the east–west ditch although this does appear to be superimposed on, or by, what seems to be a curvilinear enclosure at G. Aerial photographs of levelled sites, be they visible in crop or bare soil, very rarely show any evidence of relative chronology – nor should this be expected, especially through the medium of crops growing above them. So in the case of G it is unknown if, or which, one feature preceded another or if the map shows one contemporary system of ditches. The enclosure at G and the northern one at F are of forms that are usually accepted as of 'Iron Age and/or Romano-British' date – a mere one thousand or so years – but the southern probable enclosure at F is less-certainly attributed to a date range. However, it does appear to be attached to the linear ditch that extends to site G, so might there be a useful relationship from the linear ditch?

At its southern end the linear ditch appears to continue, or be continued by, a modern boundary. Therefore, one immediate possibility is that it is a ploughed-out post-medieval boundary, a date that seems to be enhanced by the First Edition Ordnance Survey 1:10,560 map (1866) that suggests the two parallel ditches and the continuation of one to the west may have bounded woods (W). There are, however, two points in favour of a pre-medieval date for the linear ditch. Where the linear ditch lies close to the northern enclosure at F it shows a slight curve as if it was respecting something (the enclosure) that was an extant feature in the landscape. This could suggest contemporary dates for the two features or that the enclosure had not completely been levelled by the time the linear ditch was cut. The 1886 map does not show a boundary or ditch continuing north from the modern one, only a straight footpath that lay slightly east of the ditch mapped from the aerial photographs. The second point concerns the relationship of the linear ditch to the parish boundary, or rather the lack of any relationship between the two as it could be expected that the two would be coincident where both run east to west if the linear ditch was of medieval or post-medieval date. However, broad droves of medieval date are well known and another explanation is that the parish boundary and linear ditch could have formed part of such a drove, although that would cut across another parish boundary between F and G. Reference to earlier enclosure maps may elucidate these problems in this small area.

The preceding few paragraphs are little more than a casual first attempt to begin to unravel a small part of this clay landscape and what has been done may pose more questions than it provides answers. It may, however, be those questions that provoke the next steps to be taken in this area: possibly some fieldwalking to collect surface material, perhaps examination of the enclosure maps, perhaps some small, question-led, trial trenches, and definitely more aerial photography to fill in gaps when crop conditions are suitable. The above explanation of sites and their relationships is a way towards improving our understanding anywhere that features have been mapped to depict past landscapes. Doing so on the Bedfordshire clay is something that was not possible before the 1996 aerial survey recorded a first glimpse of the density and extent of features there.

44 A sample of the small enclosures that seem consistently to be of mid-Iron Age date on the river gravels in the vicinity of Bedford. The shapes of the enclosures vary and individually would make morphological categorisation of little value. A more relevant attribute may be that they occur in small groups often with pits clustering within and around them. Several excavations, in areas that include these types of site, have recently taken place in advance of mineral extraction and has provided the dating evidence. Very little investigative work of this kind has occurred on clays. © *Rog Palmer*

10　0　　　　　　　　Metres　　　　　　　　100

IMPLICATIONS FOR ARCHAEOLOGY?

Our knowledge of settlement on river gravels can be summarised from the many excavations there and, in places, we may be able to attribute specific plan forms to a date range. For example, recent excavations in advance of mineral extraction have shown that groups of variously shaped small ditched enclosures are recurrently of middle Iron Age date in the Bedford area (44). But on the clay we have no such parallels and no current or proposed research projects aimed at clarifying what has been recorded from the air. Any advances in knowledge are likely to be derived from excavations that may occur prior to development (see Kenney; this volume). While these are providing a wealth of new and unexpected information in many parts of England there should later come a time when specific questions will be formulated that require critically placed excavation to provide answers. A priority for understanding clayland settlement would first be to interpret and accurately map all the visible archaeological sites within a defined extent of clay – such as Alison Deegan has done for Northamptonshire (this volume) – and to follow that with a series of ground investigations. Logically, these would be fieldwalking, perhaps geophysical survey at selected points and research-driven excavations that target specific types of features or groups of features. Through this we should begin to level the imbalance that archaeology on clay soils has suffered and may begin to understand past settlement on, and uses of, the clay and the relationships of its past occupants with adjacent areas.

IMPLICATIONS FOR AERIAL SURVEY

The 1996 vertical photographs of Bedfordshire have shown us that the clay can be as densely populated as 'easier' soils and so have given us a new vision of a neglected landscape zone that now requires study and understanding. To me, it has also demonstrated how inadequate our present resources and methods are for obtaining a similar photographic record of any part of the country if, or when, such dry conditions occur again. Archaeology needs an efficient method to record large areas of ground, not individual fields, when these 'once in sixty years' effects reoccur (Evans; this volume). One has only to look at the pages of, for example the issue of *Rescue News* that followed the drought summer of 1976 to be aware of the flapping wings of the observer-photographers who knew that below them had been evidence of the richest crop-marked archaeological landscape seen since (probably) 1949. Yet their funding, numbers and methods had left them impotent to record more than a sprinkling of choice sites. At present there are fewer active observer-photographers than there were in the 1970s and they now have a much wider range of duties (see Grady; this volume). In effect one person is responsible for almost all the archaeological, architectural and scenic aerial photography of England south of the Wash. It is apparent from conversations with observers and from the relatively informal series of 'flying reports' circulated by English Heritage, that recording levelled archaeology seems often to take second, or lower place, although this may not be formally acknowledged.

There *is* a solution but it will require a lot of pressure to instigate and, perhaps more importantly, a belief among our aerial specialists that it is, in fact, a solution. Observer-photographers are very aware of changing crop conditions during the summer months and interested people are kept aware of these through English Heritage's emailed reports. This knowledge could provide the key to activating more thorough aerial survey at the optimal time in areas where crops are at their most responsive above buried archaeological features.

In the past, even if such contingency funds had been successfully fought for and obtained, the problem has been the delay between commissioning a vertical aerial survey and its completion as, during summer months, the few commercial survey companies in Britain and Europe are usually fully booked and busy. However, from 2002 high-resolution images of the ground have been obtainable from commercial satellites such as QuickBird and will become of higher resolution with the next generation of WorldView satellites. Unlike aerial survey companies these satellites can be activated with minimal delay and WorldView will be able to make daily revisits to the same area. However, one currently insurmountable problem associated with commissioning satellite images is that the clarity of view, due to atmospheric haze and cloud cover, is not known until the images have been taken and examined.

The level of detail these satellites record will not match that achieved by low-flying observers' photographs of specific targets in optimum conditions, but it is debatable whether we need that detail as a base-level record. Instead, the satellite data will totally cover whole areas of land in a way which airborne observers cannot and should provide information commensurate with that required by mapping programmes such as English Heritage are currently undertaking at 1:10,000 scale. Any recording of featureless ground by these means should be seen as a bonus because, within landscape archaeology, such knowledge can be as important as that of settlement features. Archaeology needs a practical method of recording large areas of the ground on those rare occasions when weather conditions force crops to make past landscapes visible. And this needs to be done before they are ploughed out of existence. One solution for this absence of observation by archaeologists is to utilise the capabilities of the high-resolution satellites that have the ability and potential to revolutionise our capture of plough-levelled archaeological landscapes.

ACKNOWLEDGEMENTS

In preparing this short paper I am grateful to Bob Evans for discussion of crops on clay in general and for exchanging detailed comment on various aerial photographs. Dave Cowley, Damian Grady and Toby Driver have provided useful feedback about the practice of observer-directed aerial photography although they may distance themselves from opinions in this paper which are very much those of the writer.

BIBLIOGRAPHY

Allen, G.W.G. 1984. Discovery from the air. *Aerial Archaeology* 10.
Brophy, K. & Cowley, D. (eds) 2005. *From the air: understanding aerial archaeology.* Stroud: Tempus.
Crawford, O.G.S. & Keiller, A. 1928. *Wessex from the air.* Oxford: Oxford University Press.
DigitalGlobe, 2006. www.digitalglobe.com (accessed 18 September 2006).
Featherstone, R., Horne, P., MacLeod, D. & Bewley, R. 1995. Aerial reconnaissance in England, summer 1995. *Antiquity* 69, 981–88.
Hall, D. 2001. *Turning the plough: Midlands open fields: landscape character and proposals for management.* English Heritage/Northamptonshire County Council.
Hampton, J.N. 1989. The Air Photography Unit of the Royal Commission on the Historical Monuments of England 1965-1985. In D. Kennedy (ed.), *Into the sun: essays in air photography in honour of Derrick Riley*, 13-28. J.R. Collis Publications.
Mills, J. 2003. Aerial archaeology on clay geologies. *AARGnews* 27, 12–19.
Mills, J. 2005. Bias and the world of the vertical aerial photograph. In K. Brophy & D. Cowley (eds), *From the air: understanding aerial archaeology*, 117-26. Stroud: Tempus.
Palmer, R. 1996. Air photo interpretation and the Lincolnshire Fenland. *Landscape History* 18, 5–16.
Palmer, R. 2005. "If they used their own photographs they wouldn't take them like that". In K. Brophy & D. Cowley (eds), *From the air: understanding aerial archaeology*, 94-116. Stroud: Tempus.
SSEW, 1983. *Soils of England and Wales: sheet 4: Eastern England (1:250,000).* Soil Survey of England and Wales: HMSO.
Whimster, R. 1983. Aerial reconnaissance from Cambridge: a retrospective view 1945-89. In G.S. Maxwell (ed.), *The impact of aerial reconnaissance on archaeology*, 92-105. York: Council for British Archaeology Research Report 49.
Wilson, D.R. 1978. Light soils and heavy soils: a question of priorities. *Aerial Archaeology* 2, 46-49.
Wilson, D. 1995. John Kenneth Sinclair St Joseph 1912-1994. *Proceedings of the British Academy* 87, 417-36.

8

Archaeology on the Boulder Clay in Northamptonshire: some results from the Northamptonshire National Mapping Programme Project

Alison Deegan

INTRODUCTION

The Northamptonshire National Mapping Programme (NMP) Project has produced a varied and exciting digital dataset derived from mapping archaeological information that is visible on aerial photographs. Following a brief overview of the project, this chapter will use this data to examine the distribution of sites in relation to the clay lands. Specifically, it will look at the variability of crop mark distribution on the Boulder Clay and the distribution and nature of soil mark evidence. The second part of this chapter will examine the evidence from this NMP project and other sources for the exploitation of the clay lands, and, in particular, the Boulder Clay, in later prehistory and the Roman period.

BACKGROUND

This chapter draws on the work of the Northamptonshire NMP Project ('the project' hereon) and subsequent analysis of the project data. This project was conducted by Northamptonshire County Council (NCC) between 1994 and 2005 and funded by English Heritage (formerly the Royal Commission on Historical Monuments (England)). The project combined archaeological information from thousands of specialist and vertical aerial photographs into a map format that could be readily analysed against other data sets in the NCC Geographical Information System (GIS). The overwhelming majority of the specialist aerial photographs were generated by the NCC reconnaissance programme, principally by Glenn Foard (Foard, forthcoming). The NCC photographs

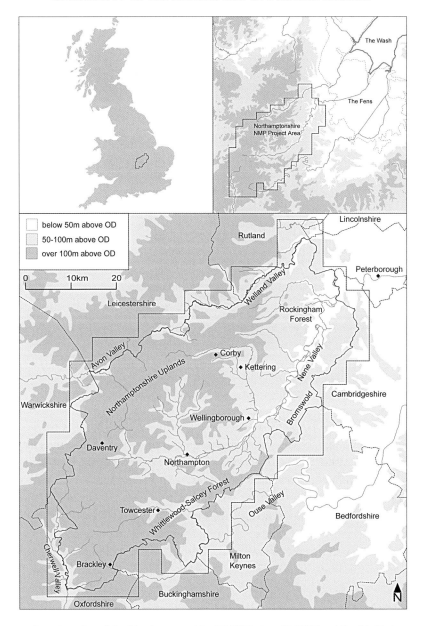

45 Location plan of the Northamptonshire NMP Project. © *NCC and English Heritage*

were often the only source of crop marks and soil marks on the Boulder Clay. A full account of the NMP project and its operation can be found in the Management Report, which is available at the Archaeology Data Service website (http://ads.ahds.ac.uk/). Publication of the project's archaeological analyses will be completed in 2007.

The project encompasses the whole of the modern county of Northamptonshire and small parts of ten adjoining counties and unitary authorities at the heart of England in the East Midlands (45).

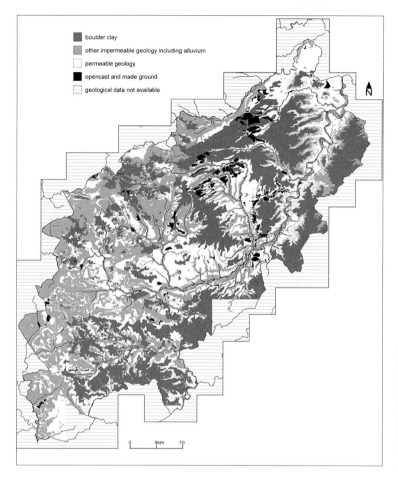

boulder clay

other impermeable geology including alluvium

permeable geology

opencast and made ground

geological data not available

46 The distribution of Boulder Clay, other impermeable and permeable geologies in Northamptonshire. © NCC and English Heritage

NORTHAMPTONSHIRE'S GEOLOGY

The surface geology of the modern county of Northamptonshire is varied and complicated. The underlying structure can be imagined as alternating layers of permeable and impermeable Jurassic and Cretaceous rocks dipping gently from the west and north-west of the county towards the south-east. In the Pleistocene great ice sheets deposited blankets of chalky, impermeable Boulder Clay across this structure, and in warmer periods, sorted sands and gravels were deposited by the glacial melt-waters (Martin and Osborn 1976). Subsequent action of glacial melt-waters and rivers cut down through the Boulder Clays and earlier rocks to expose the underlying strata, re-worked the gravel terraces and deposited alluvium on the valley floors thus producing a highly complex geological landscape (Martin and Osborn 1976). Boulder clay is thus widely distributed across the county but heavily interspersed with more permeable outcrops as well as other clays and alluvium (46).

Calculated on the maps of the British Geological Survey, just under one third of the county of Northamptonshire is covered in Boulder Clay deposits. Other impermeable

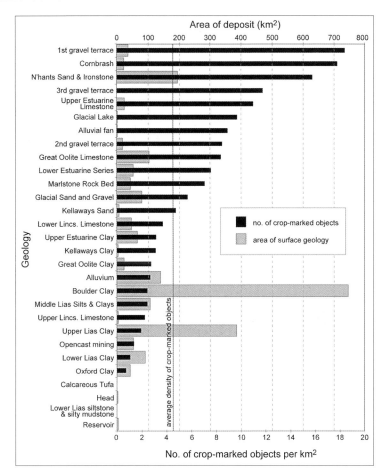

47 Total area of each surface geological strata with the average number of archaeological crop marks per km². © NCC and English Heritage

rocks, mainly Upper Lias Clay and alluvium, cover another third. The permeable strata, notably the Northampton Sand and Ironstone, outcrop over approximately 30% of the county. Data for some small areas were not available at the time of writing and a small proportion of the land surface has been disturbed.

THE DISTRIBUTION OF EVIDENCE

Within the GIS, the Northamptonshire NMP project recorded nearly 15,000 map objects. Each map object may represent features from the simplest monuments like single ring ditches up to extensive and complex field systems. Although each map object does not represent a consistent quantity of archaeology they are the best quantifiable unit that is available. These map objects are roughly equivalent to the RCHME MORPH2.2 'site' (Edis et al. 1989). Approximately 22% of these map objects were earthworks but because fewer than 2% of these are thought to date to the pre-medieval periods this discussion will concentrate on the levelled sites, recorded as both crop marks and soil marks.

As might be expected the majority of archaeological crop marks recorded by this project occurred on the permeable geologies – two-thirds in fact. However, some 17% of the crop marks occurred on the Boulder Clay and just under 15% on the other impermeable geologies. It should be noted though, that whilst the impermeable geologies produced nearly a third of all the crop-marked archaeological sites, they actually cover two-thirds of the county. It is perhaps, therefore, more relevant to use site density as a comparison. Figure 47 shows the density of crop-marked archaeological sites on each of the major deposits.

Although the Boulder Clay produced a significant proportion of the crop-marked archaeological sites the average density of those sites at 2.5 per km² is not substantially greater than the densities recorded on other impermeable geologies. Moreover, it is considerably lower than the calculations for most of the freely drained rocks; the Northampton Sand and Ironstone, for example, have an average density of 15.5 sites per km². Figure 48 illustrates that the crop-marked archaeological sites are not evenly distributed across the Boulder Clay deposits. There are very few crop-marked archaeological features recorded on the Boulder Clay in the Rockingham Forest area, but crop marks on Boulder Clay are common across the Nene-Ouse watershed where in some parishes the average density of crop-marked objects on the Boulder Clay is as high as 14 per km².

There is, however, a considerable visual difference between the best of the Boulder Clay crop marks on the Nene-Ouse watershed and those to be found on the more permeable geologies. The vague and diffuse crop marks of enclosures and boundaries on Boulder Clay in Raunds are fairly typical and it is probable that these features are far more complex than they appear (49). In contrast, the crop marks on the freely drained Northampton Sand and Ironstone show the fine details of buried enclosures, ring ditches, pits and medieval plough furrows as well as underlying geological features (50).

Returning to the variations observed across the Boulder Clay in different parts of the county, it is not clear why the Nene–Ouse watershed Boulder Clay should yield such numerous, albeit faint, crop marks and the Rockingham Forest virtually none. A comparison of the soil types arising in these two areas does not suggest a marked difference in the character of the underlying Boulder Clay. Both are covered with slowly permeable calcareous or clayey soils: Hanslope (411d) and Ragdale (712g), although the soil survey data available for this area may simply be too coarse to reveal significant localised variations (SSEW 1983). The depth of Boulder Clay and overlying soils may influence the development of crop marks; drainage may be better in areas where shallower Boulder Clay overlies more permeable strata.

Current land use is certainly a factor in the development of crop marks. Today a far greater proportion of the Nene-Ouse watershed is under arable cultivation than the Rockingham Forest (Centre for Ecology and Hydrology 2000). However, even in fields that are under arable regimes, Boulder Clay crop marks are sparse in the Rockingham Forest. Recent land use history may also be a factor. In 1928 the pioneering Land Utilisation Survey recorded the extent of arable and grassland in the county on a field-by-field basis (Beaver 1943). Figure 51 illustrates the differences in land use between Brigstock in Rockingham Forest and Raunds and Hargrave on the Bromswold in 1928. A large proportion of Brigstock lies on Boulder Clay and there are very few

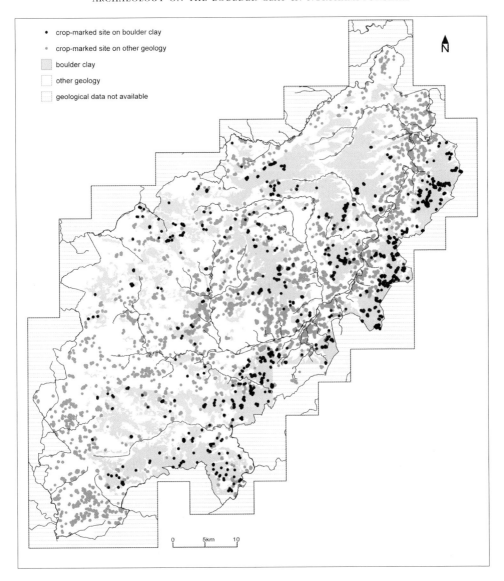

48 The extent of Boulder Clay and distribution of archaeological crop marks. © *NCC and English Heritage*

archaeological crop-marked sites. In 1928, as today, surviving ancient woodland covered a substantial area of the parish. At that time relatively few fields had been converted to arable cultivation from pasture and park land. By contrast, in 1928 large areas of the Boulder Clay in the parishes of Raunds and Hargrave were already under arable cultivation and there was relatively little woodland. It is perhaps significant that most of the Boulder Clay crop marks recorded so far have occurred in those fields that were under the plough in 1928. It is not clear whether the actual processes of cultivation have encouraged the formation of crop marks or perhaps that these fields were naturally better drained and thus more attractive to both ancient settlers and modern arable farmers.

Left: 49 Typical crop marks of possible Iron Age or Roman period boundaries and enclosures on Boulder Clay in the parish of Hargrave. *NCC TL0370/032 23/6/1995. © Northamptonshire County Council*

Below: 50 Typical crop marks of archaeological and natural features on Northampton Sand and Ironstone in the parish of Harlestone. *NCC SP7165/102 20/6/1996. © Northamptonshire County Council*

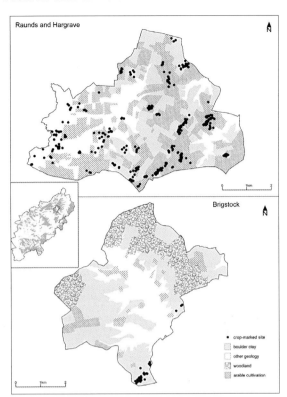

Right: 51 Land use in 1928 and the distribution of archaeological crop marks in the parishes of Brigstock in Rockingham Forest, and of Raunds and Hargrave on the Bromswold. *After Beaver 1943.* © *NCC and English Heritage*

Below: 52 The distribution of archaeological soil marks in relation to ancient woodland, medieval deer parks and charcoal burning hearths in the Rockingham Forest area. © *NCC and English Heritage*

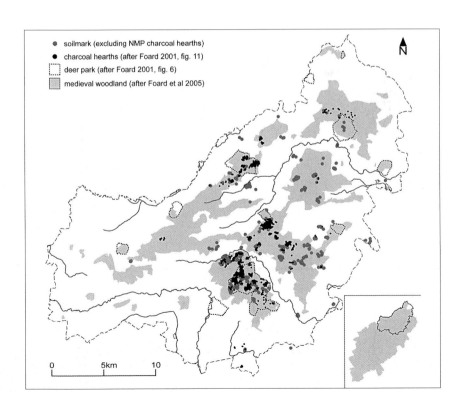

The apparent dearth of crop-marked information in the Rockingham Forest area is somewhat compensated by a minor but nonetheless significant spread of soil marks. Similar but smaller concentrations are also found in parts of the Whittlewood and Salcey Forests. Many of these soil marks are the remains of the charcoal-burning platforms of medieval and perhaps earlier date but others indicate features of later prehistoric and Roman date. These clusters of clear, well-defined soil marks only occur in certain conditions and although they are concentrated on the Boulder Clay their relationship to this deposit is only a secondary factor. Rather, the appearance of these soil marks is linked to a particular sequence of historic and present land use which was tied to the presence of these heavy, impermeable soils.

Figure 52 is a plan of the Rockingham Forest area showing the areas of ancient woodland and the extent of the medieval deer parks. These are the areas that escaped ploughing during the medieval period and survived either as woodland or pasture up to the mid-twentieth century. The pressures for arable cultivation in the medieval period had ensured that woodland and pasture were restricted to the least-productive soils: those on the heavy, poorly-drained Boulder Clay. This ensured the preservation of pre-medieval earthworks in such areas, and it is these features that now appear as well-defined soil marks. The clarity of the soil marks is due to fresh, deep ploughing and is gradually lost with subsequent ploughing. Thus, the appearance of well-defined soil marks is actually an indication of the destruction of previously well-preserved archaeology.

EVIDENCE FOR NEOLITHIC AND BRONZE AGE ACTIVITY ON THE BOULDER CLAY

Figure 53 compares three values for each major geology: the percentage of all archaeological crop marks recorded on each geology, the percentage of possible Neolithic monuments on each geology and the percentage of possible Bronze Age monuments. The Northampton Sand and Ironstone produced the greatest number of crop-marked archaeological sites and similarly the greatest number of possible Neolithic and Bronze Age monuments. The Marlstone Rock Bed, another freely draining stratum bearing acidic soils, produced fewer than 4% of all the crop-marked sites but more than one fifth of the possible Neolithic monuments such as long barrows and large circular enclosures. Mindful of the usual caveats concerning the dating of crop-marked features and the small sample size, this comparison does suggest that the Neolithic monument builders had a real preference for this geology.

It is the acidic soils of the Marlstone Rock Bed and the Northampton Sand and Ironstone that are most likely to have supported the Scot's Pine that was detected in environmental samples taken from the Redlands Farm Long Barrow on the valley floor (Campbell and Robinson forthcoming). Uniquely, amongst the trees of Mesolithic and Neolithic Britain, the pine can be killed by fire (Rackham 1996, 34). It is perhaps this advantage or even the presence of natural clearances caused by lightning strikes (Brown 2000) that made these areas popular with the earliest monument builders.

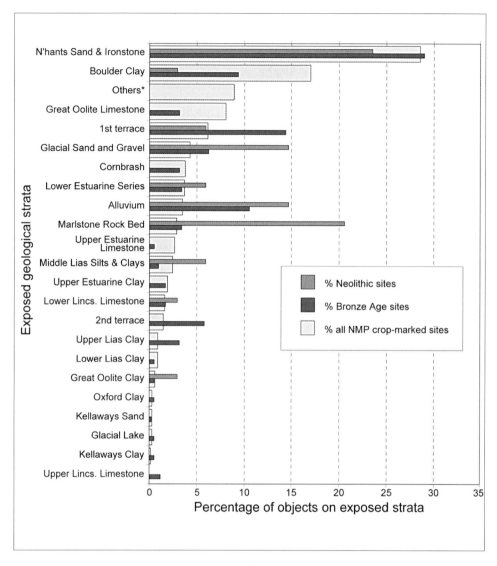

53 The distribution of ring ditches and other possible Neolithic and Bronze Age monuments compared to that of all crop-marked archaeological sites by geology (sample sizes: Neolithic = 34, Bronze Age = 418 and all crop marks = 10,744). © *NCC and English Heritage*

In contrast, the heavy soils of the Boulder Clays produced 17% of all crop-marked sites but only 9% of Bronze Age ring ditches and just one Neolithic monument, although others, of course, may remain undetected. The majority of the Boulder Clay crop marks undoubtedly indicate Iron Age and later activity.

It may be useful to compare the distribution of crop-marked features with Neolithic and Bronze Age surface finds catalogued in the Northamptonshire Sites and Monuments Record and from the fieldwalking of Martin and Hall (Hall 1985). These records suggest that one third of all Neolithic and over one quarter of Bronze Age finds and scatters were recovered from the Boulder Clay and Upper Lias Clay, suggesting that the clay lands were exploited at this time. However Hall has already observed that the geological map data does not always reflect the localised ground conditions and he maintains that, like the monuments known from air photographs, the majority of early prehistoric finds were recovered from well-drained soils (Hall 1985).

Environmental investigations associated with the Raunds Area Project indicate that the Neolithic and Bronze Age monument builders opened up the freer-draining soils of the valley floors and sides to create a mosaic of grass, regenerated scrub and surviving woodland (Campbell and Robinson forthcoming). Although there is little environmental information about the clay lands at these times, it is possible that the woodland survived over most of these areas and continued to be used for hunting and foraging.

EVIDENCE FOR IRON AGE AND ROMAN ACTIVITY ON THE BOULDER CLAY

Although they are mostly undated it is likely that the majority of crop marks recorded by the Northamptonshire NMP project relate to Iron Age or Roman activity. The forms and distributions of these features suggest long and complex sequences of development and what follows here is merely a brief summary of some of the differences observed between the permeable geologies and the clay lands.

This project has generated a significant, although undoubtedly very incomplete, record of later prehistoric open settlement in the county. Excavation has shown that some open settlements such as those at Great Oakley and Wakerley Hall Wood probably date to the Late Bronze Age and Early Iron Age, but later examples such as the Middle to Late Iron Age settlement at The Lodge, Crick are also known (Jackson 1982; 1976; Chapman 1995). Most of the open settlement recorded by the project is located on the freer-draining soils, probably because slight features such as hut circles and pit clusters rarely produce clear crop marks on the clay lands. Excavations on the valley floor at Wollaston have unravelled the development of pit- and ditch-defined land divisions and farmsteads, which were known previously from aerial photographs and mapping (Meadows 1995). This part of the valley floor appears to have been cleared of woodland during the Bronze Age, then maintained as open grassland and ultimately divided up into large rectangular blocks of land. The earliest boundaries were demarcated by pit alignments, many of which were subsequently re-cut by ditches. This framework of land division continued in use through the Iron Age when small enclosed farmsteads were built at the corners of the land parcels. Some of these settlements, or their successors, were still occupied in the Roman period.

Although crop-marked evidence for long pit alignments is largely absent from the clay lands this may not be a true reflection of their distribution. Excavations at Crick have revealed a pit alignment on Boulder Clay, and other examples may produce crop marks that look like continuous ditches or none at all (Kidd 1999, 5). Despite the absence of pit alignments, the predominantly rectilinear arrangements of boundaries, trackways and ditches that are seen on the permeable geologies are also present on the Boulder Clay.

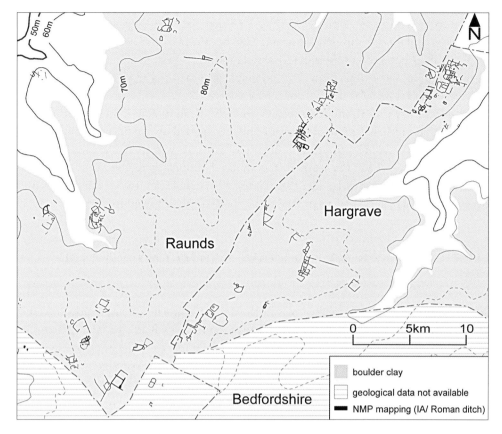

54 Extract of Iron Age and Roman period landscapes on the Boulder Clay in the parishes of Raunds and Hargrave. © *Alison Deegan*

In the parishes of Raunds and Hargrave, although evidence for long boundaries is lacking, the arrangements of the various settlement groups hint at an underlying rectilinear arrangement of land allotment (54). These landscapes are interspersed with less regular and more sinuous forms of boundaries and trackways but these are more difficult to date and some may relate to later activities such as medieval assarting.

Where the crop-mark evidence is sufficiently comprehensive it indicates that, as at Wollaston, Middle Iron Age to Roman rural settlement often developed in clusters of rectilinear enclosures built alongside the boundaries and trackways of the pre-existing land parcels. These developments can be seen on both the permeable geologies and the clay lands. The clay lands however, despite the relative inferiority of the crop-mark evidence, have produced a wider variety of enclosure types.

Figure 55 shows some of the irregular and curvilinear enclosures recorded on the Boulder Clay. The first two examples: the sub-circular enclosure at Brigstock and a similar feature at Draughton, have been excavated and dated to the Iron Age, as has one of the enclosures at Bozeat (Jackson 1983; Grimes 1961; Hall 1971). The presence of trackways and the possible banjo-enclosure may be significant to understanding the economy of the sites.

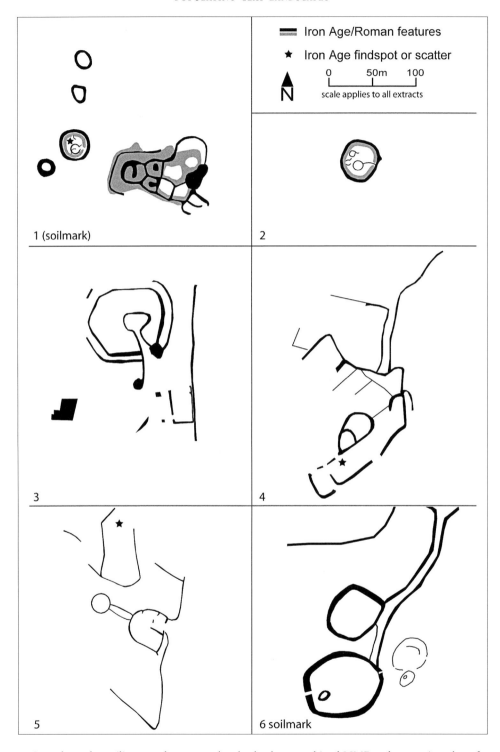

55 Irregular and curvilinear enclosures on the clay lands: 1. combined NMP and excavation plan of enclosures at Brigstock. *After Jackson 1983, figure 3*; 2. Draughton. *After Grimes 1961, figure 11.3*; 3. Bozeat; 4. Castle Ashby; 5. Brafield on the Green; 6. Bozeat. © *Alison Deegan*

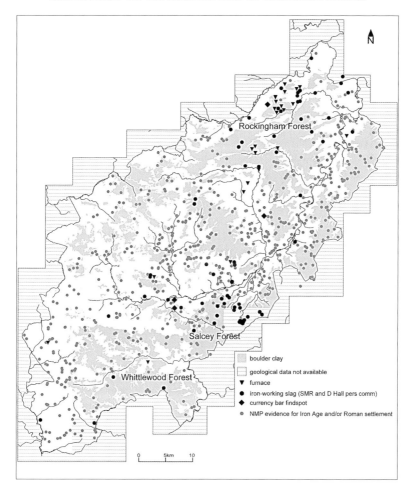

56 The distribution of Boulder Clay and Iron Age and Roman ironworking evidence in relation to settlements of those periods. © *Alison Deegan*

This NMP project has produced little direct evidence about the agricultural economy of the Iron Age and Roman periods. Ground investigations at Wollaston and Stanwick indicate that a mix of arable and pasture was practised on the valley floors (Meadows 1995, 44; Robinson 1992, 205). Jackson (1983) suggested sheep-rearing predominated on the heavy soils around the Brigstock enclosure. There and elsewhere the presence of funnel-like entrances leading into some of the enclosures may be further evidence of pastoral activities.

Other crafts and industries have left little tangible evidence that is visible as crop marks or soil marks either on the well-drained soils or the clay lands. However, evidence for iron-working, in the form of furnaces and deposits of smelting and smithing slags (mainly the latter), has been recovered from excavations and fieldwalking (Northamptonshire SMR). It is interesting to note that these are concentrated on, or at, the margins of the clay lands (56). These are generally accepted to be of medieval date although it is also possible that some of the charcoal-burning hearths may also date to these periods.

Plausibly, the clay land environments provided the resources for iron-working and/or production. Certainly iron ore was available: both as ironstone erratics within the Boulder Clay and nodular bands that were accessible by quarrying down through the clay (Bellamy *et al.* 2000, figure 3). And, of course, clay for furnace construction was widely available.

Little is known about the vegetation cover on the Boulder Clay areas during the Iron Age and Roman period but these are the areas most likely to have resisted extensive woodland clearance in the Neolithic and Bronze Age. Furthermore, Robinson has suggested that the absence of any major alluviation event on the Nene Valley floor indicates soil stability on the neighbouring watersheds through permanent grassland or even woodland (Robinson 1992, 206). However, woodland needed to have been carefully controlled and managed through coppicing to produce suitable charcoal for fuel capable of meeting the demands of both iron-working and the pottery industries that thrived in the Nene Valley.

CONCLUSIONS

To summarise, there is a not-unexpected bias in the crop mark evidence towards the better drained soils and although crop marks are less common on the clay lands there are distinct concentrations, particularly on the Nene-Ouse watershed. The pattern of Boulder Clay crop marks is complemented by minor concentrations of soil marks in the Rockingham Forest. Whilst we do not fully understand the mechanism for the appearance of crop marks on some areas of Boulder Clay but not others, an archaeological cause cannot yet be discounted. However, it is understood that the appearance of clusters of good, clear soil marks of pre-medieval remains on the Boulder Clay in the Rockingham Forest is a consequence of a specific history of land use and is, unfortunately, an indication of the loss of hitherto well-preserved earthworks.

On present evidence, the clay lands do not appear to have been extensively cleared for settlement or monument building in the Neolithic and Bronze Age, however field investigations may yet reveal evidence to the contrary. Finally, the combined evidence of the Northamptonshire NMP project and results from fieldwalking and excavation indicate that during the Iron Age and Roman periods the clay lands were exploited in diverse and varied manners. Some areas were brought under a system of rectilinear land division, whilst in others the only visible aspects are isolated curvilinear enclosures that were perhaps associated with a predominantly pastoral economy. Inferences based on a variety of sources suggest some areas were under-managed woodland that supplied the iron and pottery industries with fuel.

ACKNOWLEDGEMENTS

Northamptonshire NMP Project data reproduced with the kind permission of the joint copyright holders: Northamptonshire County Council and English Heritage. Geological data supplied and reproduced with the kind permission of the copyright holder, Northamptonshire County Council. I would like to thank Rog Palmer and Jess Mills for inviting me to contribute to this publication and Glenn Foard for our many fruitful discussions on the uses of aerial photography in Northamptonshire and the Northamptonshire NMP Project.

BIBLIOGRAPHY

Archaeology Data Service. 2006. *Northamptonshire National Mapping Programme*. http://ads.ahds. ac.uk/. Accessed 19/01/06.

Beaver, S.H. 1943. Part 58. Northamptonshire. In L. Dudley Stamp (ed.), *The land of Britain. The report of the land utilisation survey of Britain*, 331-92. London: Geographical Publications Ltd.

Bellamy, B., Jackson, D. & Johnston, G. 2000. Early iron smelting in the Rockingham Forest area: a survey of the evidence. *Northamptonshire Archaeology* 29, 103-28.

Brown, A.G. 2000. Floodplain vegetation history: clearings as potential ritual spaces? In A.S. Fairbain (ed.), *Plants in Neolithic Britain and Beyond*, 49-62. Oxford: Oxbow.

Campbell, G. & Robinson, M. forthcoming. Environment and land use in the valley bottom. In J. Harding & F. Healy, *Rounds Area Project: the Neolithic and Bronze Age landscapes of West Cotton, Stanwick and Irthlingborough, Northamptonshire*. English Heritage.

Centre for Ecology and Hydrology, 2000. *Land cover map 2000*. Centre for Ecology and Hydrology.

Chapman, A. 1995. Crick. *South Midlands Archaeology* 25, 37-9.

Edis J., MacLeod, D. & Bewley, R.H. 1989. An archaeologist's guide to the classification of cropmarks and soilmarks. *Antiquity* 63, 112-26.

Foard, G. forthcoming. Aerial reconnaissance in Northamptonshire. In A. Deegan & G. Foard, *Mapping Ancient Landscapes in Northamptonshire*. English Heritage.

Grimes, W.F. 1961. Settlements at Draughton, Northants, Colsterworth, Lincs and Heathrow, Middlesex. In S.S. Frere (ed.), *Problems of the Iron Age in Southern Britain*, 21-28. Institute of Archaeology Occasional Paper No. 11.

Hall, D.N. 1971. Pre-Roman Iron Age sites at Bozeat. *Bedfordshire Archaeological Journal* 6, 17-22.

Hall, D.N. 1985. Survey work in Eastern England. In S. Macready & F.H. Thompson (eds), *Archaeological field survey in Britain and abroad*, 25-43. The Society of Antiquaries of London. Occasional Paper (New Series) VI.

Jackson, D.A. 1976. Two Iron Age sites north of Kettering, Northamptonshire. *Northamptonshire Archaeology* 11, 71-88.

Jackson, D.A. 1982. Great Oakley and other Iron Age sites in the Corby area. *Northamptonshire Archaeology* 17, 3-23.

Jackson, D.A. 1983. Excavation of an Iron Age site at Brigstock, Northants. *Northamptonshire Archaeology* 18, 7-32.

Kidd, A. 1999. *An archaeological resource assessment of the Later Bronze and Iron Ages (the first millennium BC) in Northamptonshire*. East Midlands Archaeological Research Framework. www.leicester.ac.uk. Accessed 19/01/05.

Martin, R.A. & Osborn, G. 1976. An outline of the geology of Northamptonshire. *Northamptonshire Natural History and Field Club*. Geological Section.

Meadows, I. 1995. Wollaston. *South Midlands Archaeology* 25, 41-5.

Rackham, O. 1996. *Trees and woodland in the British landscape: the complete history of Britain's trees, woods and hedgerows*. London: Pheonix.

Robinson, M. 1992. Environment, archaeology and alluvium on the river gravels of the south Midlands. In S. Needham & M.G. Macklin (eds), *Alluvial archaeology in Britain. Proceedings of a conference sponsored by the RMC Group plc 3-5 January 1991*, 197-208. Oxford: Oxbow.

Soil Survey of England and Wales (SSEW), 1983. *Soils of England and Wales: Sheet 4, Eastern England*. 1:250,000. Harpenden.

9

A banjo enclosure and Roman farmstead: excavations at Caldecote Highfields, Cambridgeshire

Scott Kenney

INTRODUCTION

Recent excavations at Caldecote Highfields, 9km to the west of Cambridge, revealed a hitherto unknown banjo enclosure. Although such features have been identified from crop marks as far north as Cleveland and Yorkshire, most examples are concentrated in the southern counties of England, with the greatest number found in Hampshire. Very few of these sites have been investigated and even fewer been excavated. At Caldecote, the banjo enclosure was replaced by a Roman farmstead that may have included a vineyard.

Over two seasons in 2000 and 2001, Cambridgeshire County Council's Archaeological Field Unit (CCC AFU) conducted excavations on the claylands to the east of Highfields Road, Caldecote, Cambridgeshire (TL35405880; 57). This area of settlement is relatively modern and has always been separate from the older village core to the south. The work was carried out for JS Bloor Homes Ltd and Wilcon Homes Ltd.

An aerial photographic assessment in 1996 gave no indication that extensive remains lay within this expanse of clay. The potential of the site was, however, revealed by evaluation trenching during 1996, which suggested that Iron Age and Roman occupation sites had survived in the form of roundhouse gullies, enclosure systems and pits.

GEOLOGY AND TOPOGRAPHY

According to the British Geological Survey (BGS 1975), the site lies on Pleistocene Boulder Clay overlying the Upper Cretaceous Gault Clay. The Boulder Clay in this area

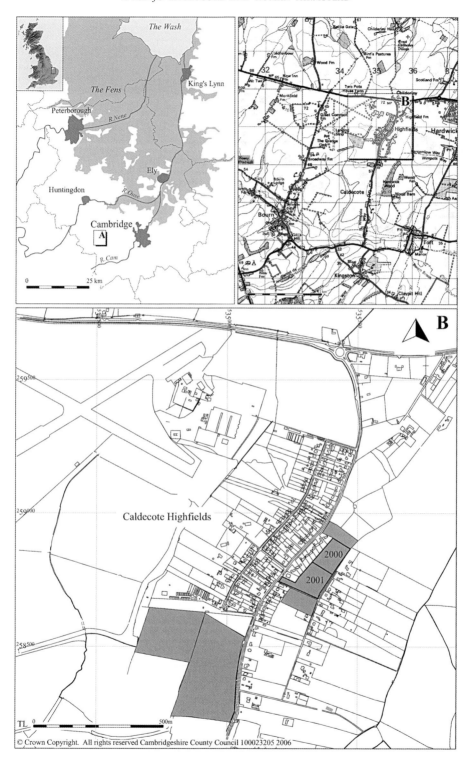

57 Site location plan. Toned areas were evaluated in 1996 by CCC AFU. Caldecote Highfields excavation areas are labelled by year. © *CCC AFU*

is riddled with veins and patches of gravels and sand, and contains numerous geological erratics including sandstones and limestones. During the excavations, it rapidly became apparent that the site quickly waterlogged and some form of drainage was a necessity for living and working on this land. In each season of excavation, a small shallow lake formed in the southern corner of the site, and did not drain until the area had to be pumped for backfilling.

The site is located on some of the higher ground in the parish at between 66-69m OD. As with the land to the north of the site, the ground slopes down from north-east to south-west.

LANDSCAPE, HISTORICAL AND ARCHAEOLOGICAL BACKGROUND

By the time that housing development was advancing in Caldecote and neighbouring parishes during the 1990s, the once widely-held notion that there was no prehistoric settlement on heavy clay soils had lost its credibility. Many sites had been excavated around Cambridgeshire and throughout the Midlands that disproved this former hypothesis. For example, the new housing development at Cambourne which lies 3km to the west of Caldecote has recently been subject to archaeological investigation. A series of excavations carried out by Wessex Archaeology has revealed evidence of Bronze Age, Iron Age and Roman occupation on the Boulder Clay.

There are no entries in the Cambridgeshire Historic Environment Record (CHER) for Caldecote pertaining to finds from the Palaeolithic, Mesolithic, Neolithic and Bronze Age periods, while evidence for the Iron Age and Romano-British periods is relatively limited. Approximately 700m to the south-west of the subject site, excavations in 1997 uncovered evidence of the local Roman field system, as well as three phases of hitherto undiscovered Late Iron Age agricultural features. The Roman ditches produced pottery dating to the second to fourth centuries AD. The density of artefacts in ditches within the northern part of the field suggests that the focus of Roman settlement was probably located towards the northern part of Highfields.

Various soil marks and crop marks of medieval ridge and furrow agriculture around Highfields have been recorded from aerial photographs (CHER 0192, 11434, 11435). A review of the aerial photographic evidence available for Highfields was undertaken in 1996 by Air Photo Services. This revealed clear evidence of medieval ridge and furrow on a broadly east to west alignment. Earthworks of putative house platforms are recorded from the southern end of Highfields (CHER 11226, 11225), while evidence of medieval settlement was excavated to the south-west of the subject site by CCC AFU in 1997.

Caldecote was mentioned in Domesday and the spelling of the name was identical to the modern one: the name means 'cold cottages' and was probably intended as a term of reproach (Reaney 1943). The village is strung out along what was the Kingston to Childerley road, formerly known as Strympole Way. Caldecote village proper is largely focussed around the church near the Bourn Brook. The more recent development at Highfields is located approximately 2.5km north of the church.

Recorded in Domesday as having a population of 15 in 1086, Caldecote followed a national trend of increasing agricultural prosperity and growing populations rising to a peak in the thirteenth and fourteenth centuries, followed by a dramatic and drastic decline. In 1377, 78 people in the parish contributed to the poll tax, but by 1554 the population had slumped to nine householders. The small population recorded during the medieval period persisted so that an estimate of the population in 1728 was 15 families. Thereafter a gradual rise took place until there were 144 residents in 1851. Agricultural depression in the later nineteenth century was the probable reason for further decline and it was only when twentieth-century development in the Caldecote Highfields area took place that earlier population levels were regained. By 1911 the population had reached 160 and thereafter it has risen steadily (VCH 1973, 17).

Information from the Cambridge Record Office (CRO) indicates that before enclosure, Caldecote had three open fields, of which the most northerly – Dams (or North) Field covered much of the area to the west of Highfields Road (CRO 296/P8). At the time of enclosure Dams Field was common pastureland. The land to the east of the road was divided into enclosures around Highfields Farm, owned by Clare College. The ownership of the subject site was not mentioned.

Caldecote parish was enclosed by an award of 1854 and it was only at this time that the road from the parish centre was extended northwards to join the St Neots to Cambridge road (the modern A428). Formerly Broad Way, this is now called Highfields Road, but until the building of houses in Highfields at the beginning of this century the roads east, south and west from Caldecote remained the main arteries for the settlement and Broad Way constituted little more than a track. The enclosure awards map (CRO Q/RDc 76) shows that the field boundaries established in 1854 have largely persisted. The pattern of settlement in Caldecote parish has changed markedly in this century since a speculator brought a strip of land in Highfields and divided it into small parcels for development by self-supporting smallholders. Growth accelerated in 1932 with the development of more plots with bungalows (VCH 1973, 17-19).

The most notable, and unexpected, result of the historical research at Caldecote is the discovery that the existing fields have occupied almost the same areas and boundaries since 1854. The creation of such large fields at enclosure may be a product of the relatively late date of the award or the underlying clay geology that could have been unsuitable for arable exploitation without the provision of an expensive drainage system, which would be more economically justified when applied to a large field.

MESOLITHIC FLINT TOOLS

The recent archaeological investigations have produced two Mesolithic artefacts: a narrow flint tranchet axe and a utilised blade. The tranchet axe or adze represents an example of a characteristic Mesolithic tool type and the utilised blade would be compatible with such a date. Tranchet adze/axes were used throughout the Mesolithic and the date range of c.8000–4000 BC cannot be further refined. Both pieces were recovered from

Iron Age or later features and are clearly residual. There is little published evidence of Mesolithic activity in the vicinity of the site, most work in the region having tended to concentrate in and around the fen margins and islands. Recently, evidence of Mesolithic activity in the form of short stay camps has been identified to the south-east 10km away at Trumpington and there is little reason to doubt that similar early prehistoric clayland activity may have been fairly extensive throughout the region.

A BRONZE AGE AUROCHS?

A badly preserved fragment of a bovine distal humerus was found in a pit at the southern edge of the site. Too large to belong to a domestic animal from prehistoric or Romano-British periods, its size is comparable to the undomesticated aurochs (*Bos primigenius Bojanus*). It was possible to take two measurements on this bone, one of which is far greater than that obtained from large Late Neolithic to Romano-British assemblages from Cambridgeshire studied by Ian Baxter (Baxter 1998; 1999; 2000a and b) and is well within the range for aurochs. The latest radiocarbon date for aurochs in Britain is 1629 BC obtained from material found at Blagdon in Somerset (Clutton-Brock and Burleigh 1983).

THE BANJO ENCLOSURE AND ASSOCIATED SETTLEMENT

English Heritage defines a banjo enclosure as 'a monument consisting of a small (generally less than 100m diameter) subcircular enclosure with a narrow approach way consisting of parallel ditches (thus banjo shaped)'. This does not specifically include the presence of a house within the main enclosure and as such, those banjo enclosures that do contain a structure may have had a different function from those that lack one. Several shallow irregularly shaped pits and hollows pre-dated the initial phase of the Caldecote enclosure, close to the southern side of the entrance. Their function remains uncertain, although they contained pottery, implying nearby occupation.

Several phases of the banjo enclosure system were uncovered at Caldecote, all of which date to the Late Iron Age. The initial phase comprised a ditch with generally a V-shaped profile up to 0.9m deep around the sub-triangular main enclosure (58, A). Within the enclosure was a single roundhouse with its entrance facing north-west, looking down the entrance corridor. In common with subsequent phases, the entrance corridor ditches were not continuous. Each phase of the main enclosure did not quite meet the entrance passage ditches on either side, and other gaps existed further along.

The enclosure was later enlarged by expanding towards the north-east, while the recut ditch was shallower and had a more rounded profile than the previous phase (58, B). Two sickle-shaped ditched features lay just outside the enclosure to the south-east during this phase. Subsequently, the banjo enclosure ditch was re-established very much to its original plan and almost to its original depth; slight modifications were introduced to the main enclosure entrance with short out-turned 'horns' being created and the

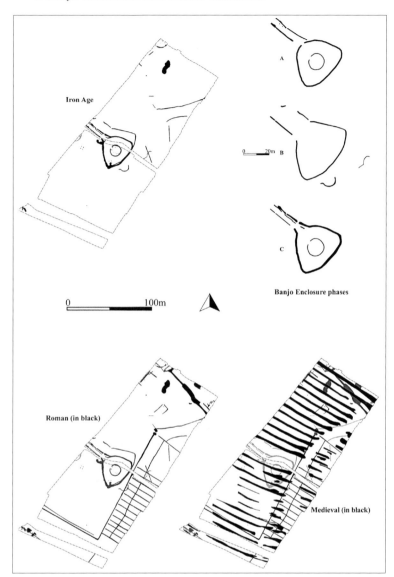

58 Iron Age, Roman and medieval phase plans, with detail of banjo enclosure subphases. © CCC AFU

addition of a fenceline along the inside of the entrance corridor on its north-eastern side (58, C).

The final phase was marked by destruction: infills were black in many places with charcoal and fragments of burnt daub seen throughout, but most prominently on the north-eastern side. A large pit was later dug into the southern corner of the enclosure ditch, possibly as a well. The pit had a shallow metalled ramp running down into it from the north. Within the fills of the pit were fragments of an almost complete rotary quern stone, while placed on the base of the pit was a large unworked quartzitic boulder.

At the extreme northern edge of the site was another roundhouse, 13m in diameter, surrounded by small ditch or gully features. Between this and the banjo enclosure lay a trackway, demarcated by parallel flanking ditches. A third roundhouse, 15m in diameter, lay just to the west of the banjo enclosure with a four-post structure positioned close to it: such posts in a square arrangement are a common feature of Iron Age sites and are often interpreted as the foundations for grain stores.

Some 623 sherds of Iron Age pottery (4.474kg) were recovered from the site (59), the most important single source being the ditch of the banjo enclosure, which produced 119 sherds (1.388kg). The gullies and internal post-holes of round houses were also significant sources of material. A research agenda for the Iron Age in eastern England (Brown and Glazebrook 2000) has called for the publication of quantified pottery assemblages and remarked on the lack of such reports: very little Iron Age pottery has in fact been published from south Cambridgeshire over the last 25 years. The sheer diversity of fabrics – 19 in all – at Iron Age Caldecote suggests that several sources of supply are represented. The forthcoming full publication of the Caldecote material will therefore make a significant contribution to current research into Iron Age ceramics. The decline in the incidence of grog-tempered pottery at pre-Roman Caldecote is remarkable: for the first time in Late Iron Age East Anglia, this site demonstrates that, after an initial and apparently whole-hearted adoption of 'Belgic' pottery, the vogue for this new pottery passed and the existing Middle Iron Age tradition reasserted itself with some vigour.

Six large pieces of quern were recovered representing a maximum of five querns. The stone came from a variety of sources, some of which lie close to Caldecote and others that were some distance from the site (the latter including greensand from the quarry site on the Hythe Beds at Lodsworth, Sussex). The placing of quern fragments into features cut into ditches may have been an important element in marking (or renewing) boundaries. Querns also appear to have been placed in the entrances of buildings. The presence of special deposits within site boundaries is well attested and may act as a symbolic marker between wild nature outside and organised habitation inside (Hill 1995).

The faunal assemblage from Iron Age features is dominated by sheep/goat, which account for 48% of the main domesticates. Cattle comprise 22% and pigs 20% respectively of the main domestic species. The cattle bones derive from both juvenile and adult beasts, while most sheep were slaughtered before their second year. Pig remains are relatively frequent and these animals must have been around two years old when they were slaughtered. The bones recovered are consistent with domestic pigs, with nothing to suggest the presence of wild specimens. Equid fragments account for 9.5% of bones identified to domestic species. The morphology of the teeth and the post-cranial remains indicates that these derive from pony-sized equines (*Equus caballus*). Ages at death range between less than 4½ years and 10 years.

In addition, two worked bone objects came from Iron Age contexts. One was made from a sheep/goat tibia shaft with the distal end shaped and smoothed to form a gouge, while the other was a juvenile cattle ulna with the distal shaft shaped and smoothed to form an awl.

The excavation of the almost complete ground-plan of a previously unknown banjo enclosure will add greatly to the corpus of work on this monument type, providing an example far to the north of the main distribution. The distinctive shape of the Caldecote enclosure may indicate a regional variation.

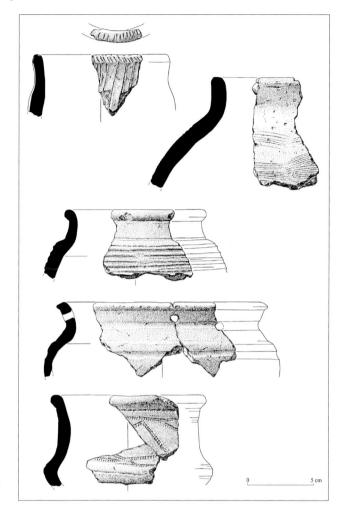

59 Selected sherds of Iron Age
pottery. © *CCC AFU*

THE ROMAN FARMSTEAD

Post-dating the banjo enclosure, although not directly overlying it, a Roman farmstead
dating to the first to the second centuries AD was established (*58*). This consisted of a large
ditch running NW–SE forming part of a large, probably rectangular enclosure, within
which were further linear and potentially rectilinear features. One small rectangular
arrangement of narrow shallow ditches enclosed two small post-holes or pits, the smaller
of which contained 17 sherds of a decorated Nene Valley flagon. This vessel may once
have held a cremation and the feature may have been a funerary structure.

  Across the south-eastern part of the site lay 14 parallel ditches running WNW-ESE and
terminating to the west within one metre of a perpendicular bounding ditch. This group
of features is reminiscent of the pattern found at Wollaston in Northamptonshire, which
has been identified as a Roman vineyard (Meadows 1997). The example at Caldecote is
physically almost identical in size, spacing and arrangement to that at Wollaston and has

thus been provisionally given the same interpretation. Elsewhere within Cambridgeshire, at the Milton East Waste site and St Neots Love's Farm excavations, morphologically similar examples have been found (Connor 1999; Hinman pers. comm.), although the former is thought to be Iron Age, rather than Roman. It is possible that the western boundary ditch at Caldecote was first established for at least part of its length during the Iron Age and recut during the Roman period.

Elsewhere on the site, the earliest Roman features appeared to be quarries, although one of these may have originated in the Late Iron Age. Environmental evidence suggests that these features were allowed to fill very slowly but may have contained standing water for much of their existence. Given the rather impermeable nature of the local geology, this is not surprising and the features may have been created specifically as watering holes. Another possibility is that they were dug to extract clay and/or the sand that occurs occasionally in veins through the Boulder Clay, and only served as watering holes when quarrying had ceased.

Towards the end of the Roman period, the agricultural system seems to have been abandoned, although elements of it became fossilised as boundaries to a trackway. A few pits were also dug at this time, some of which seem to relate to the earlier boundary ditches by 'capping' them at an existing terminus. The excavations yielded an assemblage of 1634 sherds of Roman period pottery (15.453kg). Study of the material suggests that the possible vineyard was laid out c.AD 125 and had become derelict by c.AD 250.

The few fragments of animal bone recovered from Romano-British deposits suggest that cattle were now the most frequent domestic species. Sheep were much less common than in the Iron Age and pig numbers are even further reduced. The reduction in numbers of the latter, if not merely a product of small sample size, suggests increased deforestation in the immediate area of the site as pigs were customarily sent to forage in adjacent woodland until the end of the medieval period. Isolated teeth of field vole were found, suggesting open grassland.

Very little environmental evidence was recovered with most of the charred remains coming from Roman contexts. The evident lack of charred cereal remains may indicate an absence of settlement or grain processing in the vicinity. When combined with evidence from the mollusca, a short-lived settlement may be suggested. The presence of freshwater molluscs suggests damp conditions and possibly some localised flooding.

The existence of a first- or second-century farmstead at Caldecote Highfields is not unexpected, given the proximity of a road to the north (A428) thought to have Roman or earlier origins. What is more unusual is the presence of an agricultural system that may have been a vineyard. The animal remains suggest that cattle may have been kept as livestock, while the local environment became more open and greater clearance took place.

MEDIEVAL AND LATER LAND USE

The site provides a useful overview of the local medieval ridge and furrow pattern, including a headland that conformed to the route of the prehistoric trackway (58). This headland was still clearly visible as a low earthwork bank before stripping of the site began. It changed direction at the same point as the ancient trackway, and the width of the gap between the furrow ends mirrors the spacing of the trackway ditches. This suggests that the trackway survived as a route or boundary feature until the medieval period and was then preserved beneath the bank of the headland. The modern field boundaries do not conform to the former medieval headland alignment.

Susan Oosthuizen (2003) has proposed a link between the prehistoric and medieval field systems in West Cambridgeshire, with particular reference to the Bourn Valley. The results of the Caldecote excavations seem to support this theory, with one boundary or routeway persisting from at least the Iron Age until the medieval period.

INTERPRETATION: LATER PREHISTORIC LIFE ON THE CLAYLANDS

Despite the apparently simple description cited earlier, there is great variation in both the size and shape of banjo enclosures. While many have quite circular or subcircular main enclosures, some are D-shaped, subrectangular or irregular and complex. The same level of variation exists in the interrelation of the Banjo to its surroundings. In some cases the Banjo entranceway ditches turn sharply outwards after some distance, forming a trackway or boundary, in the latter case sometimes curving back to form a larger enclosure. The subcircular enclosure can be as much as 90m in diameter or as small as 35m; the Caldecote example measures 41m x 32m during its smaller phases and 51m x 32m during its expanded middle phase. The entranceway ditches are also usually continuous, unlike the Caldecote example, where it might be imagined that the gaps were for the movement of livestock.

The banjo enclosure at Micheldever Wood in Hampshire is the best example published so far of the excavation of this type of monument (Fasham 1987). Although there are some similarities to the Caldecote example, the Micheldever Wood Banjo does not contain a roundhouse. When that report was published, only 55 examples of the monument type were recorded; this has now risen to 112, and there seems to be no reason why the number should not continue to rise.

In terms of landscape associations, the banjo enclosure entrance points north-west, possibly towards a small watercourse running perpendicular to that line. There is however, a source of water much closer to hand to the southeast, so this is probably not the reason for this. It is now known that there was contemporary settlement in the area of Cambourne, only a few kilometres to the west, and the route of the A428 was probably in use as a track before the Roman period.

The trading associations of this settlement are clearly shown from the pottery assemblage, and this indicates contact with contemporary settlements and passing traders. This would not be possible unless there was proximity to a main routeway bringing such trade from further afield. The people here and at Cambourne must have known one another, even if their affiliations differed, and it is likely that they would have interacted. The Cambourne settlement was larger and Caldecote may have been an outlier of the community.

Although a certain amount of clay is a necessary component of a functional topsoil for agricultural purposes, too high a proportion will result in boggy, poorly-draining fields. This is not to say that agriculture cannot take place on such soils, but it is difficult to work. At Caldecote during the Late Iron Age, there seems to have been a definite preference for the raising of livestock as opposed to horticulture. While this might bear out the notion of a lack of pre-Roman agriculture on clay soils, the inhabitants of the Caldecote site seem to have managed quite well at their chosen trade.

Elsewhere in Cambridgeshire, Iron Age settlements have been located strung out along river valleys, which may in themselves have acted as routeways. More recent examples, particularly those found on the claylands have been located closer to arterial trackways that become part of the Roman road system. Whether this is coincidental is open to debate, but if the higher ground where the trackways run is composed of clay, then settlements located to exploit trade routes will, of necessity, also be located on the clay.

Considering all of the points made above, it seems clear that the claylands did have advantages over better draining soils for some Iron Age communities and that future excavations will reveal the extent to which this is the case. When the Romans came to Britain and observed the ways in which the native population were perhaps failing to fully exploit the heavy soils in some areas, it appears they decided to apply their own agricultural expertise. Whatever crops were grown on the Caldecote site, it would seem that this enterprise was at least moderately successful, as shown by the hints of wealth in the pottery assemblage.

CONCLUSIONS

Excavations at Caldecote Highfields have added crucial new information to the distribution map for banjo enclosures and offer the tantalising possibility that a regional sub-form has been identified. The author suggests that should any more be discovered with a triangular enclosure that the name Balalaika Enclosure be considered, as a nod to the Russian instrument of the same name and shape.

On a more serious note, analysis of the Iron Age pottery assemblage has yielded a most surprising result. Middle Iron Age-type pottery is most common in the first and last phase of the banjo enclosure, but Late Iron Age grog-tempered wares are more prevalent during the middle phase. This suggests that the types of ceramics found on sites in the Late Iron Age may be influenced by the ebb and flow of trade and tribal affiliation as much as by what is most current.

The Roman phase of the site has yielded another example of a type of agricultural system that has had several potential explanations proposed. Some excavators have argued for a simple raised bed cultivation system while others have suggested a specialist use for asparagus or vines. The vineyard explanation is favoured by the current author, remembering that grapes were not only grown for winemaking, but also ended up on the Roman table.

Lastly, the excavations have shown that the influence of some features of the later prehistoric landscape persist until post-medieval Enclosure, affecting the placement of settlement and routes between them.

ACKNOWLEDGEMENTS

The author wishes to thank JS Bloor Homes Ltd and Wilcon Homes Ltd for funding the excavations. Paul Spoerry and Stephen Macaulay managed the project for the CCC AFU. Thanks are also due to the field team for their hard work, and the illustrators, particularly Carlos Silva, who produced the pottery figure. Specialists who reported on the various materials were: Ian Baxter (faunal remains), Barry Bishop (flints), Sarah Percival (querns), Paul Sealey (pottery) and Chris Stevens (environmental). Liz Popescu did initial edits and gave much helpful advice. Rog Palmer supplied much needed encouragement and suggestions.

BIBLIOGRAPHY

Baxter, I.L. 1998. *Landwade Road, Fordham (FOR LR 96). Report on the animal, bird and amphibian bone*. Unpublished report, CCC AFU.

Baxter, I.L. 1999. *Greenhouse Farm, Fen Ditton (FDI GF 96). Report on the mammal, bird, amphibian and fish bone*. Unpublished report, CCC AFU.

Baxter, I.L. 2000a. *Babraham Road, Cambridge (CAM BAB 97-98). Report on the animal bones*. Unpublished report, CCC AFU.

Baxter, I.L. 2000b. *Report on the mammal and bird bones from Haddon Lodge Farm, Cambridgeshire*. Unpublished report, CCC AFU.

British Geological Survey 1975. *1:50000 series sheet 187, Huntingdon, drift geology*. HMSO.

Brown, N. & Glazebrook, J. (eds) 2000. Research and archaeology: a framework for the eastern counties 1: research agenda and strategy. *East Anglian Archaeology Occasional Papers* 8.

Clutton-Brock, J. & Burleigh, R. 1983. Some archaeological applications of the dating of animal bone by radiocarbon with particular reference to post-Pleistocene extinctions. In W.G. Mook & H.T. Waterbolk (eds), *Proceedings of the first international symposium 14C and archaeology*, 409-19. Council of Europe PACT 8.

Connor, A. 1999. *Iron Age settlement and agriculture at Butt Lane, Milton*. Unpublished report no. 157, CCC AFU.

Fasham, P.J. 1987. A banjo enclosure in Micheldever Wood, Hampshire. *Hampshire Field Club Monograph* 5.

Hill, J.D. 1995. *Ritual and rubbish in the Iron Age of Wessex*. Oxford: British Archaeological Report.

Meadows, I., 1997. Wollaston: the Nene Valley, a British Moselle? *Current Archaeology* 150, 212-15.

Oosthuizen, S. 2003. The roots of the common fields: linking prehistoric and medieval field systems in West Cambridgeshire. *Landscapes* 4:1, 40-64.

Reaney, P.H., 1943. *The place-names of Cambridgeshire and the Isle of Ely*. English Place-Name Society No. 19, Cambridge.

VCH, 1973. *Victoria histories of the counties of England: Cambridgeshire V, West Cambridgeshire: Longstow and Wetherley hundreds*. Oxford: Oxford University Press.

10

Surveying the claylands: combining aerial survey and fieldwalking methods in identifying archaeological sites on 'difficult' soils

Jessica Mills

INTRODUCTION

Employing archaeological techniques on clay soils and geologies is notoriously fraught with difficulty. With soils and geologies being heavy-going and more susceptible to waterlogging and drying-out, the usual battery of archaeological methods quite often struggle to identify archaeological sites. Aerial survey is frequently unproductive over clay soils as crops usually fail to indicate any traces of buried features. Geophysical survey can be inconsistent and the practicalities of archaeological excavation can become arduous with heavy clay soils constantly changing from being wet and sticky to cracked and dried-out. Fieldwalking remains the easiest option in locating archaeological remains on the claylands, however, the inherent biases of this methodology (which relies on individuals being able to notice artefacts in the ploughsoil) dictate that solely using this technique is very problematical.

With all these caveats in mind, it is the aim of this paper to examine the best approach to identifying archaeological sites on the claylands. With the use of two clayland study areas in Bedfordshire, I will demonstrate how a combination of techniques, in particular aerial survey and fieldwalking, provides the best methodology for rapidly assessing the archaeological potential of clay landscapes. The results provided in this paper will show that clay soils and geologies are not as barren as they first appear and that significant variation in the ways in which different techniques reveal archaeological information on the clays needs further assessment. Finally, this research has opened up new questions concerning the settlement and chronology of clay landscapes in this area.

METHODOLOGICAL CONTEXT

Surveying clay landscapes is by no means as straightforward as investigating, for example, a river valley or chalkland environment. First, aerial survey quite often fails to identify archaeological sites. The reasons for this are not yet fully understood, but a number of different suggestions have been put forward (see Evans; this volume; Mills 2003). There are two main forms of aerial survey currently utilised in Britain today that result in either oblique or vertical photographs. Oblique photography entails taking photographs from an angle which focus closely on an archaeological feature. The methodology is reliant upon the photographer observing archaeological phenomena. Whether or not photographs are taken of features depends upon the research agenda, interests and targets of the photographer. In contrast, vertical photography is commissioned by an individual (see Coleman; this volume) and records areas of the landscape from a vertical viewpoint usually covering a larger area than oblique photography. As the camera is mounted in the aircraft and not held in the hand of the photographer, the taking of photographs is automatic and does not rely on human judgement. The output comprises sets of geographically unbiased photographs of large areas of the landscape, which may or may not contain archaeological evidence.

Aerial photography undertaken during the summer relies on changes in crop growth such as colour and height to indicate the presence of buried features. Factors such as soil moisture content, soil depth, nutrients, time of year and type of soil/geology all affect the way a crop develops (see Evans; this volume). Over features that have been cut into the subsoil such as ditches and pits, crops tend to grow taller, stronger and take longer to ripen due to increased moisture and nutrients trapped in the below-ground features (Wilson 2000, 67-70). However, crop development suffers if there is too much or too little water within the soil, with plants eventually dying. Consequently, the way in which soils and geologies hold water greatly affects how crops may reveal buried features. Geologies such as sands, gravels and chalk are free-draining and promote changes in crop growth much more readily than clay geologies which retain water for very long periods of time (Jones & Evans 1975). Therefore, the kind of soils and geologies a crop is planted in plays a very important role in whether or not buried features may become visible from the air. With clay soils and geologies retaining water for longer periods of time than other geologies as well as becoming regularly waterlogged, it is not surprising that clay landscapes infrequently reveal archaeological crop marks.

This inconsistent way in which crops on clay soils and geologies show archaeological sites from the air has ensured that over the years, aerial survey (in particular oblique photography) has concentrated on the bountiful sands, gravels and chalklands of Britain. Such concentrated effort to record the large numbers of archaeological crop marks that appear frequently in these areas has led to a dearth of aerial reconnaissance over the claylands. Again, with minimal archaeological aerial survey being undertaken over the clays, few sites have been found re-affirming the idea that clay soils and geologies were largely unsettled in the past. Nevertheless, despite much archaeological aerial survey ignoring the vast tracts of clay in favour of chalklands and river valleys, the deployment of vertical photography which covers large blocks of land irrespective of geology has captured snapshots of clayland activity in a way that oblique photography has struggled to do. For example, Bedfordshire County Council regularly commissions vertical aerial surveys of the county and through doing so has been able to record a much greater number of archaeological sites on clay landscapes than with any other aerial reconnaissance method (Mills 2003; 2005; Palmer 2005 and this volume). In particular, the 1996 Bedfordshire survey which was flown during optimal conditions for revealing archaeological crop marks on clay (see Evans; this volume) recorded an unprecedented number of archaeological sites (Mills 2003). So, despite clay soils and geologies revealing archaeological sites under quite particular conditions, greater aerial reconnaissance is needed over the claylands to be able to take advantage of these circumstances thus increasing the chances of finding new sites.

The advantages of using aerial photography as a means for recording clay landscapes are numerous despite the above caveats. For instance, such surveys are able to rapidly record archaeological sites over a wide area and provide information such as the form and distribution of sites. But despite aerial survey providing a swift means for surveying large areas, it does lack the ability to provide detailed chronological and artefactual information. Therefore, a complementary ground-based technique is needed which can rapidly assess landscapes – and systematic fieldwalking provides the best answer. Artefactual data recovered from the ploughsoil may provide information on site chronologies, types of activities undertaken as well as point to aspects of trade and exchange. It is this kind of information that adds new dimensions to the spatial perspective of sites obtained from aerial photographs.

Significantly, however, fieldwalking may provide an alternative distribution of archaeological material within a landscape that may not be obtainable from aerial photography (see Kiarszys et al.; this volume). As stated earlier, aerial survey over clay soils and geologies can be variable at best and requires particular conditions for crops to reveal below-ground archaeological features. Therefore, aerial photographs usually show only a partial picture of clayland settlement and use. By integrating fieldwalking techniques sites may be discovered which will not show up from the air, indeed many past activities may not have resulted in the digging of features into the ground-surface. Conversely, many tasks may have resulted in no artefactual information being deposited into the ground, leaving aerial survey as a means by which to identify such activity. Such reasons dictate, therefore, that just employing one technique when surveying clay landscapes will result in erroneous distributions and interpretations of clayland settlement.

The next section of this chapter will outline a programme of research conducted on the north Bedfordshire claylands. This research utilised aerial photographic and fieldwalking data as an efficient and informative methodology for rapidly ascertaining the general nature of clayland settlement and chronology over a large area. This research has revealed that the claylands of north Bedfordshire were extensively settled from later prehistory onwards and that the ways in which different clay geologies respond to archaeological survey may introduce significant biases into the interpretation of clayland site distributions.

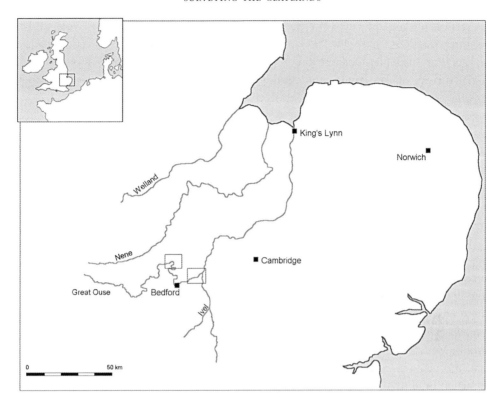

60 Location map showing both study areas. © *Jessica Mills*

RESEARCH CONTEXT

Two study areas within the claylands of north Bedfordshire were selected for archaeological assessment (*60*).

Study area one covers a 90sq km zone of clay 'upland' and river valley focusing on the confluence of the rivers Great Ouse and Ivel at Tempsford (NGR TL161534). Study area two lies to the west of study area one and focuses on a 72sq km section of the Great Ouse river valley and its clay environs at Sharnbrook (NGR TL010590).

Through incorporating not only large expanses of clay interfluve but also the river valley of the Great Ouse, the opportunity to examine a variety of geologies and landforms was facilitated. This enabled comparisons between the archaeology of clay soils and geologies with the river gravels within the Great Ouse Valley. Indeed, prior to the 1996 vertical aerial survey of Bedfordshire, the clayland distribution of archaeological sites was deemed sporadic and small-scale (Simco 1973). Previous research on the prehistoric archaeology of the area has remarked upon the numerous and extensive crop-marked complexes on the valley gravels and lack of similar evidence for the large areas of clay (Field 1973; Green 1973; Woodward 1978). However, this picture has developed over many years through the taking of oblique photographs that have focused primarily upon the bountiful river valley gravels. As the claylands have been seen as unlikely to be subject to settlement, relatively little was known about the past settlement of this area until the 1996 vertical aerial survey.

Both study areas are predominantly rural supporting cereal production and a small number of market gardens. Due to the percentage of land under the plough (there is little woodland and limited pasture) the potential for detecting archaeological crop marks is good.

GEOLOGY AND SOILS

Consideration of the geology and soils is important in understanding crop mark formation and archaeological site distributions (see below). The study areas comprise drift deposits of alluvium, river and glacial gravels along the floodplains and river terraces (Green 2000, 9-11). These superficial deposits laid down during the Quaternary period, provide calcareous gley soils of the Mead series and gleyed brown earths of the Biggleswade and Milton series. These are generally fertile, well-drained soils used for both cultivation and pasture (King 1969). Study area two contains significant zones of Cornbrash and Great Oolite limestone where the path of the Great Ouse has, over millennia, cut into and exposed the underlying well-drained limestone bedrock. Well-drained, calcareous soils of the Moreton series predominate over these riverine geologies (SSEW 1983).

Outside of the river valleys, the most widely occurring sub-drift deposit is the Jurassic Oxford Clay (Edmonds & Dinham 1965). Within both study areas it is greatly concealed by glacial and river deposits such as Boulder Clay and gravels. The Boulder Clay comprises a calcareous drift found in large zones within both study areas. It is not wholly impermeable and is characterised as a stiff grey clay, often with inclusions and largely derived from Jurassic clays and Gault (King 1969, 6). The parent material gives rise to gley soils of the Hanslope association which are classed as being slowly permeable calcareous clayey soils (SSEW 1983). Notably, there are significant drift-free tracts of Jurassic Oxford Clay in the east and south of study area one and the valley sides of the Great Ouse in study area two. The Oxford Clay, a very heavy dark brown formation, is virtually impermeable and of low value for ground water supplies. It is very finely grained and pure with little or no inclusions (Edmonds & Dinham 1965; Rigg 1916). Its soils are of a calcareous gley variety, typically Evesham 3 and Denchworth, which are both slowly permeable soils prone to seasonal waterlogging (SSEW 1983).

SURVEY RESULTS

The 1996 vertical aerial survey of Bedfordshire was used as the primary dataset as this collection of photographs revealed an unprecedented number of archaeological sites on the claylands (see Coleman and Palmer; this volume). This was augmented by oblique photographs from the Unit for Landscape Modelling at Cambridge as well as photographs taken by local fliers. For study area one only aerial photographic data was available for analysis as no fieldwalking had been conducted in the area. However, study area two was chosen as it has been extensively fieldwalked by the archaeologist David Hall (Hall & Hutchings 1972). Analysis of two study areas, one of which having been subject to fieldwalking, has enabled an assessment of both survey techniques and their differential abilities to identify archaeological sites on clay soils and geologies.

Study area one

In total, 301 archaeological sites were noted for the 90sq km study area (*61*, Table 7). Observing the geological location of archaeological crop marks, a number of general trends have been revealed. The more productive geologies within the study area such as the river gravels contain the highest number of sites (159) and site types. These deposits form the low-lying floodplains and terraces of the rivers Great Ouse and Ivel and are well-drained fertile zones.

Boulder and Oxford clays within the study area contained fewer sites than may be expected for the percentage of land that they cover. Despite the large areas covered by these formations, only 61 sites were located on the Boulder Clay and 33 on the Oxford Clay formations. This result remains unsurprising because of the abundance of targeted oblique photography that has concentrated on the productive river gravels. Importantly, the Oxford Clay formations contained half the number of expected sites and significant tracts of this geology contained no crop-marked sites at all. This phenomenon is witnessed on the Oxford Clay plains to the east and south of the study area. From the archaeological crop mark plot (*61*), one can see that crop marks on the Boulder Clay occur in a fairly widespread distribution and large areas where they do not occur are attributable to modern development. In contrast, many of the crop marks on the Oxford Clays are close to the boundaries with the river gravels. Moreover, there are significant areas of Oxford Clay that do not reveal archaeological crop marks and these areas today are regularly ploughed agricultural lands.

Noting this differential response to aerial survey by the Oxford and Boulder Clays within the study area, it becomes imperative to determine the potential reasons why this might be occurring as it holds great implications for interpreting aerial surveys over clay geologies. Could the low number of archaeological crop marks, crop mark-free areas and crop marks on geological boundaries indicate that the Oxford Clay was deemed too heavy and waterlogged for settlement in the past? Alternatively, these areas may have been settled and utilised to a greater degree than we think, however, due to geological conditions such activity on the Oxford Clay may have left little trace upon the ground which is visible from the air.

Whatever the reasons for this distinct variation between the two different types of clay, this phenomenon has potential implications for understanding the evidence from clayland aerial survey. Therefore, study area two was examined to see if the same phenomena occurred and whether fieldwalking elicited any greater information for the Oxford Clay than is available from aerial photographs. The questions arising from this potential difference between the Boulder and Oxford Clay will be examined in more detail below.

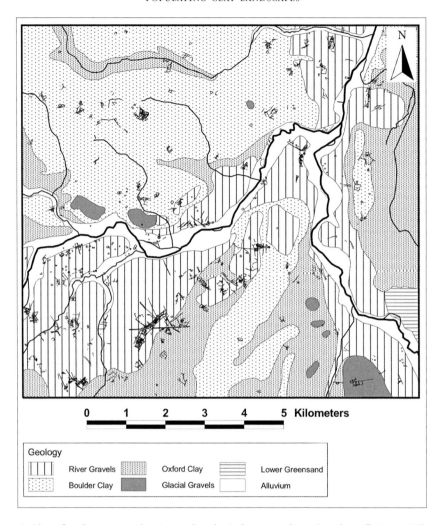

61 Plot of study area one showing archaeological crop marks and geology. © *Jessica Mills*

Geology	No. of observed sites	% of total study area	No. of expected sites
Boulder Clay	61	36.15	109
Oxford Clay	33	21.86	66
Glacial Gravels	3	1.75	5
River Gravels	159	28.78	87
Alluvium	45	10.79	32
Lower Greensand	0	0.67	2
	301	100	301

Table 7 The expected number and observed number of archaeological crop marks per geological formation in study area one

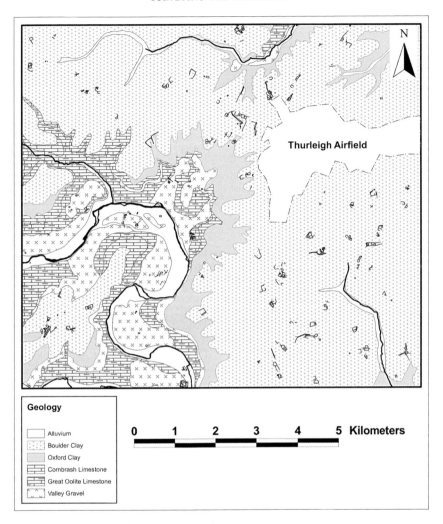

62 Plot of study area two showing archaeological crop marks and geology. © *Jessica Mills*

Geology	No. of observed sites	% of total study area	No. of expected sites
Boulder Clay	79	65.63	73.51
Oxford Clay	3	9.0	10.08
Alluvium	6	5.86	6.56
Great Oolite Limestone	5	8.24	9.23
Cornbrash Limestone	0	2.37	2.65
Valley Gravels	19	8.90	9.97
	112	**100**	**112**

Table 8 The expected number and observed number of archaeological crop marks per geological formation in study area two

Study area two

A total of 112 archaeological sites were identified on aerial photographs (*62, Table 8*) within the 72sq km study area and 31 from David Hall's fieldwalking survey (*63*). Again, comparing the location of archaeological crop marks with geology we see that river valley formations such as the gravels, limestone and alluvium account for a great number of sites – the river valley clearly being a focus for activity in the past.

Significantly, however, archaeological crop marks located on the clays, especially the Boulder Clay, show a large number of sites, spread extensively. This suggests an interfluve landscape just as busy as the river valley. Looking at the different clays in detail, again, the Boulder Clay reveals pockets of activity all over the formation. The Oxford Clay contains much fewer sites and these do appear to focus on the boundaries of this geology. So, again, within study area two, the Boulder Clay reveals more sites on aerial photographs than the Oxford Clay.

With these results, the next step was to determine whether this difference between the distribution of archaeological sites on the Boulder Clay and Oxford Clay was genuine. People in the past may have been utilising these clay geologies in different ways and to different extents, or the results may be the product of methodological bias. To help answer this question I compared the results of David Hall's fieldwalking survey with the archaeological crop marks found in study area two. It was hoped that this would help mitigate the problems inherent with ascertaining clayland site distributions from just aerial photographs.

The fieldwalking distribution shows a pattern of sites spread over the whole study area, with many sites located on the clays (*63*). At the time David Hall was fieldwalking the majority of the sites he discovered had not been recorded on aerial photographs. It was not until the 1996 vertical survey, during the very dry summer, that some of the sites discovered on the ground in the early 1970s were seen for the first time on aerial photographs. Notably, however, over one third of the fieldwalked sites still do not show up on aerial photographs whatsoever, which is quite a large proportion. Consequently, only a partial picture of clayland settlement is revealed when analysing aerial photographs. Interestingly, the fieldwalked sites located on the clays do not appear to show any major preference for clay type. There are more sites located on the Boulder Clay but this formation covers the largest area.

Of the sites discovered by fieldwalking, 61% were found to be in 'association' with features visible on aerial photographs (association taken here to mean within a 200m radius of the archaeological crop mark). Bearing in mind the difficulties in determining terms such as 'association', 'on-site' and 'off-site' as well as how far artefacts travel within the ploughsoil (Boismier 1997; Schofield 1991), 200m was decided as justifiable on the grounds of it being a likely intermediate limit around a focus of activity. So whether the activities which generated the artefactual material recovered where 'on-site' or 'off-site', up to 200m beyond the crop mark has the capacity to encompass both. Through linking the fieldwalking data to archaeological crop marks, information about chronologies and kinds of activities can be determined that is not usually available from sites recorded on aerial photographs. The artefactual and chronological information gained from the fieldwalking survey will be discussed in more detail below.

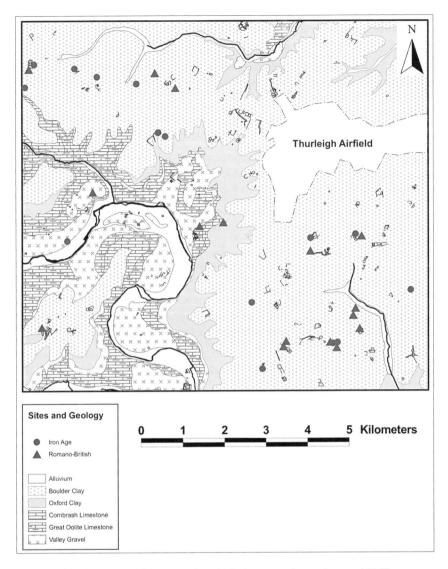

63 Plot of study area two showing archaeological crop marks, geology and Hall's fieldwalked sites. © *Jessica Mills*

COMPARISONS BETWEEN BOTH STUDY AREAS

Differences in the degree to which the Boulder Clay reveals archaeological crop marks in study area one and study area two can be elicited. In study area one, the number of sites identifiable on aerial photographs on the clay falls short of the expected number for the percentage of land that it covers (see *62*). However, in study area two, the number of archaeological crop marks exceeds the number of sites one would expect to see on the Boulder Clay (*Table 8*). With both study areas lying close together, this was investigated further to determine why archaeological crop marks were more likely to show up in study area two.

Potentially, differences in topography and elevation may hold the answer. Both study areas comprise similar arable zones with cereals forming the main crop type, however, the topography and elevation vary between both study areas. Within study area one, elevation averages 25-30m OD and the topography is gently undulating with many places being quite flat. In contrast, study area two lying to the west contains a much more varied topography with higher Boulder Clay hills and steeper hill-sides with elevations up to 90m OD. In both study areas many of the Boulder Clay crop marks lie on the tops of hills and ridges – places which are more likely to be better-drained and subject to plough erosion (see Clark & Dawson 1995). Possibly, therefore, study area one with its flatter, lower-lying topography may be revealing fewer archaeological crop marks because soils are more prone to waterlogging and less likely to suffer from erosion. Alternatively, however, the distribution may reflect real differences in the past settlement of these two areas. Study area two may have been more popular although as both study areas lie close together, this explanation does seem too simplistic.

DIFFERENCES IN CLAY GEOLOGIES

Ascertaining why crops on clays, in particular Boulder and Oxford Clay, reveal archaeological sites to differing extents remains important as it holds implications for undertaking and interpreting archaeological survey.

Significantly, there appears to be a difference between Boulder Clay and Oxford Clay formations in promoting crop growth above archaeological features. Previously, aerial archaeologists have treated all clays as being less favourable for producing crop marks, nevertheless, this research has shown that this may not be the case. The 1996 vertical aerial photographs used for this research were taken during an extremely dry summer. This has revealed many unknown sites on the Boulder Clays in both study areas but this phenomenon has not occurred to the same degree for the Oxford Clay formations – for example, at Marston Vale, a large expanse of Oxford Clay in mid-west Bedfordshire (Shotliff & Crick 1999, 32).

The physical composition of both clays and their overlying soils may hold the answer. The glacially-deposited Boulder Clay of the study area is characterised as a stiff grey clay, largely derived from Jurassic clays and Gault and containing varying amounts of sub-angular flints, pebbles and rounded chalk fragments (King 1969, 6). In contrast, the Jurassic Oxford Clay of the region comprises very finely grained and pure clay with greater impermeability than the Boulder Clays and is therefore more subject to waterlogging (Edmonds & Dinham 1965; Rigg 1916, 395). The soils that derive from the Oxford Clay, such as Evesham 3 and Denchworth, are classified by the Soil Survey of Great Britain (1983) as slowly permeable and seasonally waterlogged. Therefore, the increased amounts of inclusions within the Boulder Clay may have made soils easier to work and better drained making them more attractive for settlement.

Alternatively, it is possible that people in the past were using the Oxford Clay to a greater extent than we think. Certainly, at Marston Moretaine, mid-Bedfordshire and

Norse Road near Bedford, Iron Age settlement has been excavated on the Oxford Clay (Shotliff & Crick 1999; Edgeworth 2001). As the clay is very pure and with few inclusions the infill of ditches and other negative features will be similar to the surrounding soils making any sites more or less 'invisible' from the air and from geophysics. Moreover, the long retention of water within the Oxford Clay may be suppressing plant growth over negative features through a lack of oxygen in the rooting zone (Jones & Evans 1975, 2-3), again, enhancing the invisibility of features. Furthermore, the reason why many archaeological crop marks show up on the boundaries between the Oxford Clay and other geologies may be because these areas are stonier and freer-draining than the highly impermeable core zones of the clay.

CLAYLAND SETTLEMENT AND CHRONOLOGY

From the evidence of both study areas and published reports of the small number of excavations that have been undertaken on the Bedfordshire claylands, it was from later prehistory onwards that people began to engage with the claylands in an extensive, locally-intensive and 'visible' way (Dawson 2000a; 2000b; Edgeworth 2001; Hall & Hutchings 1972; Shotliff & Crick 1999). The digging of ditches, pits and building of structures increase the visibility of activity on the claylands – something which is missing from earlier periods in prehistory. Indeed, fieldwalking and excavation have determined a Mesolithic, Neolithic and Bronze Age background 'noise' comprising lithics (Hall & Hutchings 1972; Hall 1991; Jane Timby pers. comm.). Not surprisingly, such evidence is not visible from the air, which highlights the potential for under-representing the degree to which earlier prehistoric people were utilising the claylands. This also argues for the increased fieldwalking of the claylands to record such ephemeral settlement.

The fieldwalking evidence from study area two indicates that it was from the Early Iron Age onwards that activity on the clay gathered momentum. This increase in the intensity of tasks would have been set against a long-standing history of people living and moving on the clays. With no palaeoenvironmental data for the Bedfordshire clays, it remains impossible to determine the degree to which Mesolithic, Neolithic and Bronze Age people manipulated the dense clay woodlands. However, small-scale clearance and the exploitation of natural clearings must have been important factors in tasks conducted on the clay. So, it is within such a backdrop of small patchworks of cleared woodland that the use of the claylands intensified by the Early Iron Age.

The Iron Age sites identified by David Hall in study area two largely comprise scatters of pottery and/or burnt material (Hall & Hutchings 1972). Crop marks for which Iron Age evidence has been provided by Hall's fieldwalking suggest that small, aggregated curvilinear enclosures predominated during the Iron Age. At a few of these enclosure complexes Romano-British pottery has also been discovered indicating a continuity of settlement in certain areas. There are a number of Iron Age findspots which do not correlate with any archaeological crop marks which signifies either sites not yet visible from the air, or zones of artefactual material that are not associated with structural features. The aggregated enclosures suggest lifeways which revolved around animal husbandry, garden plots and woodland management. The small nature of the complexes as well as the general lack of trackways/droveways implies that stock-keeping and horticulture were small-scale and non-intensive. Significantly, similar Iron Age enclosures occur within the river gravels of the Great Ouse Valley. How the clayland sites relate to these valley examples remains very difficult to determine without further excavation. Were these potentially mutually exclusive groups utilising differing environs, or were people regularly moving between the river valley and clay interfluves with their animals as part of task-specific mobilities?

Romano-British settlement evidence abounds on the claylands. Where findspots correspond to archaeological crop marks in study area two, enclosures are slightly bigger with some incorporating trackways/droveways. There are many more examples of such complexes which are undated, although on morphological grounds could be Romano-British (64). Trackways can be seen to lead down off the higher Boulder Clay to small watercourses. The increase in size, complexity and the inclusion of trackways/droveways in a number of these sites suggest that more animals were being kept. As a consequence, access to fresh water would have become an increasing issue as intensification progressed. Other activities such as the grinding of cereals can be ascertained from quern stones and at one site in the parish of Souldrop, ceramic production can be elicited from ceramics, kiln bars, roof tiles and wasters (Hall & Hutchings 1972, 11). With increased Romano-British activity on the claylands, bigger settlement complexes and more varied tasks being undertaken, larger areas of woodland would needed to have been cleared. However, the extent to which woodland remained on the claylands by the end of the Romano-British period remains difficult to ascertain with no paleoenvironmental evidence.

The extensive use of both study areas continued to the end of the medieval period with many isolated farmsteads, moated sites and small villages occupying the Boulder Clays (Hall & Hutchings 1972). A large number of these villages are still in existence today, although there are numerous examples of deserted and shrunken villages.

CONCLUSIONS

This research has shown that the traditional view of clay geologies and soils being unfavourable for past settlement is completely erroneous. Throughout the past, the clay interfluves of this Bedfordshire region have been subject to activity and this substantially increased from the Early Iron Age onwards. Tasks revolving around animal husbandry, woodland management, small-scale arable cultivation, pottery production and general domestic activities were undertaken on the claylands. By the Romano-British period, clayland activities intensified with bigger and more complex enclosure systems.

This paper has also highlighted the need for an integrated approach to archaeological survey on the claylands. With significant flaws in the way aerial survey detects sites on the clays, the deployment of complementary techniques such as fieldwalking are necessary. Whilst morphological analysis of archaeological crop marks may give a general understanding of

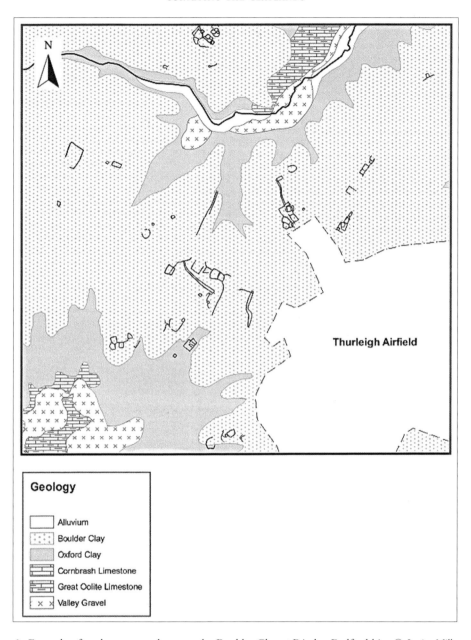

64 Example of enclosure complexes on the Boulder Clay at Riseley, Bedfordshire. © *Jessica Mills*

broad time periods of settlement, obtaining artefactual data from the claylands is imperative to verify chronologies. The importance of combined aerial and fieldwalking techniques on the claylands needs to be realised, as the opportunities for undertaking excavation (whether research- or developer-led) still remain somewhat limited for clayland areas. This being said, more research-driven projects need to focus on clayland archaeology as this remains a poorly researched and under-represented facet of past settlement.

BIBLIOGRAPHY

Boismier, W.A. 1997. *Modelling the effects of tillage processes on artefact distributions in the ploughzone.* Oxford: BAR.

Clark, R. & Dawson, M. 1995. Later prehistoric and Romano-British landscape in mid-Bedfordshire. In R. Holgate (ed.), *Chiltern archaeology: recent work. A handbook for the next decade*, 56-68. Dunstable: The Book Castle.

Dawson, M. 2000a. The Ouse Valley in the Iron Age and Roman periods: a landscape in transition. In M. Dawson (ed.), *Prehistoric, Roman and post-Roman landscapes of the Great Ouse Valley*, 107-30. York: CBA.

Dawson, M. 2000b. *Iron Age and Roman settlement on the Stagsden bypass.* Bedfordshire Archaeology Monograph 3: Bedfordshire County Council.

Edgeworth, M. 2001. An Iron Age and Romano-British farmstead at Norse Road, Bedford. *Bedfordshire Archaeology* 24, 1-19.

Edmonds, E.A. & Dinham, C.H. 1965. *Memoirs of the Geological Survey of Great Britain: geology of the country around Huntingdon and Biggleswade.* London: HMSO.

Field, K. 1973. Ring ditches of the Upper and Middle Great Ouse Valley. *Archaeological Journal* 131, 58-74.

Green, C. 2000. Geology, relief and Quaternary palaeoenvironments in the basin of the Ouse. In M. Dawson (ed.), *Prehistoric, Roman and post-Roman landscapes of the Great Ouse Valley*, 5-16. York: CBA.

Green, H.S. 1973. Early Bronze Age burial, territory, and population in Milton Keynes, Buckinghamshire and the Great Ouse Valley. *Archaeological Journal* 131, 75-139.

Hall, D. 1991. Field surveys in Bedfordshire. *Bedfordshire Archaeology* 19, 51-56.

Hall, D. & Hutchings, J. 1972. The distribution of archaeological sites between the Nene and Ouse Valleys. *Bedfordshire Archaeology* 7, 1-16.

Jones, R.J.A. & Evans, R. 1975. Soil and crop marks in the recognition of archaeological sites by air photography. In D.R. Wilson (ed.), *Aerial reconnaissance for archaeology*, 1-11. York: CBA.

King, D.W. 1969. *Soils of the Luton and Bedford district.* Special survey no. 1. Harpenden: Agricultural Research Council.

Mills, J. 2003. Aerial archaeology on clay geologies. *AARGnews* 27, 12-19.

Mills, J. 2005. Bias and the world of the vertical aerial photograph. In K. Brophy & D. Cowley (eds), *From the air: understanding aerial archaeology*, 117-26. Stroud: Tempus.

Palmer, R. 2005. 'If they used their own photos they wouldn't take them like that'. In K. Brophy & D. Cowley (eds), *From the air: understanding aerial archaeology*, 94-116. Stroud: Tempus.

Rigg, T. 1916. *The soils and crops of the market garden district of Biggleswade.* Cambridge: Cambridge University Press.

Schofield, A.J. (ed.), 1991. *Interpreting artefact scatters: contributions to ploughzone archaeology.* Oxford: Oxbow.

Shotliff, D. & Crick, J. 1999. Iron Age settlement within the Oxford Clay Vale at Beancroft Road, Marston Moretaine. *Bedfordshire Archaeology* 23, 32-42.

Simco, A. 1973. The Iron Age in the Bedford region. *Bedfordshire Archaeology* 23, 32-42.

Soil Survey of England & Wales (SSEW), 1983. *Sheet 4: Eastern England.* Harpenden.

Wilson, D.R. 2000. *Air photo interpretation for archaeologists.* 2nd edition. Stroud: Tempus.

Woodward, P.J. 1978. Flint distribution, ring ditches and Bronze Age settlement patterns in the Great Ouse Valley. *Archaeological Journal* 135, 32-56.

11

Claylands archaeology: summary and prospect

Patrick Clay

INTRODUCTION

This chapter examines the evidence presented at the Populating Clay Landscapes conference, with a particular emphasis on how recent work has changed our understanding of clay landscapes. It looks at the themes that were raised during the conference including visibility, preconceptions, biases in the record, and the wide variety of different clay soils. The potential for further research of clayland landscapes is examined and suggestions made over how this often 'hard to reach' evidence is approached.

This summary is from the perspective of a 'terrestrial' archaeologist with a particular interest in prehistoric archaeology. My knowledge of aerial archaeology and its potential, however, had been enhanced by flights and conversations with Jim Pickering. When I started my eponymous interest in the occupation and exploitation of clay soils over twenty years ago I never thought I would see a conference dedicated to the subject and would have been even more surprised that it was organised by an aerial archaeologist's group. In the early 1980s clay soils were still generally regarded as inconducive for the development of crop marks above archaeological features. However, the first excavation I directed on clay substrata as part of a 'prehistoric claylands project' in 1983 was of an Iron Age settlement at Enderby, Leicestershire which had been located during aerial reconnaissance by Jim Pickering. Unusually, this settlement was located through two enclosures showing as parch marks on pasture (65; Clay 1992; Meek *et al.* 2004).

The papers presented at the conference organised by the Aerial Archaeology Research Group show how many advances have been made in the study of clay substrata and aerial archaeology since then. The papers followed three themes – an examination of

65 Iron Age enclosures visible as parch marks in pasture fields at Enderby, Leicestershire. *Photograph: courtesy of the Jim Pickering Collection; Leicestershire County Council*

the techniques used by aerial photographers and how they can be used in the context of clay soils; an examination of some case studies of survey work and results of research and fieldwork on clay soils.

Among the points made by speakers were the relevance of different clay substrata and the importance of Potential Soil Moisture Deficit to the production of crop marks above sub-surface features. Crops on clay soils have been found to indicate archaeological sites later in the growing season than those on non-clay soils (R. Evans; this volume). This was emphasised in Bedfordshire where vertical aerial photography had been undertaken periodically since 1968, but where one survey in July 1996 had totally transformed the distribution pattern of prehistoric enclosures in the county where they were now revealed on the higher clay plateaux close to headwaters and spring sources (Coleman; this volume). Observer-directed surveys undertaken by English Heritage showed the need to balance monitoring clay soils with time and costs and suggested that this could be done when flying for other purposes (Grady; this volume).

Three contributions considered the bias introduced by 'traditional' archaeological survey and our currently-accepted ways of working. Artefact distributions and road line assessments provided a case to test whether aerial survey results were representative in parts of Scotland. Elsewhere in Scotland examination of flight paths showed that 'honey-pot' areas, where crop marks were known to appear, were overflown far more regularly than the apparent blank areas, so serving to reinforce the bias (Cowley and Dickson; this volume).

Bias and preconceived ideas were a major factor in the national survey carried out in Poland, with an aim of locating the archaeological sites within the entire country. That survey, which was started in 1990, was also biased against locating sites on heavier soils and the fieldwalking methodology was modified to be less intensive in these areas. Aerial reconnaissance had also concentrated in the river valleys but had recorded some sites on the heavier soils much to the surprise of other Polish archaeologists who were sceptical of their validity (Kiarszys, Rączkowski and Żuk; this volume).

The outstanding results from the 1996 Bedfordshire survey were compared to those from observer-directed photographs taken by Cambridge University and the Royal Commission on the Historical Monuments of England between 1945 and 1996. In a 90-minute period, the 1996 photographs had completely changed the distribution patterns of a 300sq km area of Bedfordshire and Cambridgeshire and suggested that traditional observer-directed surveys used in most of Britain and Europe may have consistently provided an inaccurate representation of past land use and settlement (Palmer; this volume). These imbalances need to be addressed.

A series of case studies began with some results from the Northamptonshire claylands following the English Heritage National Mapping Programme. Iron Age and Romano-British settlements have been revealed on the Boulder Clay interfluves between the Nene and the Ouse. Their distribution was uneven but did show concentrations while the earliest evidence appeared to be of Late Bronze Age date (Deegan; this volume).

Three sites in Cambridgeshire showed evidence that short-stay visitations in the Neolithic and Bronze Age developed into Late Bronze Age land organisation. This contribution showed the need to look at claylands within the context of other geologies and not to over emphasise their importance. Access to water was a more important factor than the underlying substrata in dictating areas for settlement while areas of clay, which could be identified through observation of tree throws, provided an important potential resource for pottery production (Christopher Evans conference paper). An example of the difficulties of working on clay sites was seen in the excavation of a 'balalaika'-shaped enclosure at Caldecote in Cambridgeshire. There, the transition between Iron Age and Roman occupation was examined in a landscape that had remained relatively unchanged from the late Bronze Age (Kenney; this volume). This paper highlighted the variety of different clay soils as did the next which studied an area of clayland in Bedfordshire. Results were compared from aerial and fieldwalking surveys and reiterated that these two survey techniques provided different, but sometimes complementary information (Mills; this volume).

RECURRENT THEMES

Preconceptions

The conference highlighted a series of issues which need to be addressed when examining clayland landscapes. Fundamental to these was the legacy of preconceptions which still persist in some areas. Claylands had long been considered to have undergone little settlement during prehistory (Fox 1932; Woodridge and Linton 1933; Clark 1945). W.G. Hoskins considered the Midlands to have been avoided by prehistoric settlers and only became densely settled in the medieval period. This is exemplified by his assessment of Leicestershire, which he described as 'a county, perhaps characteristic of the inner Midlands as a whole, which under natural conditions was very largely a region of thickly forested and heavy clays. This inhospitable landscape attracted early man only in small numbers, and even the Romans made comparatively little impression on it … The human history of Leicestershire only really begins in the second half of the fifth century (AD) with the penetration, by the first waves of Anglian settlers, along the larger rivers and to some extent along the Roman roads' (Hoskins 1957, 2). This view of minimal occupation of heavier soils was to continue into the 1980s (e.g. Tinsley 1981, 249; Turner 1981, 264). In the East Midlands, based on fieldwalking surveys in Northamptonshire, David Hall concluded that 'experience has shown that sites earlier than the Iron Age *do not* (my emphasis) occur on clay soils' and based on this he suggested modifying fieldwalking techniques to examine areas with clay soils with a less intensive method than for non-clay soils (Hall 1985, 28). The conference paper by Lidia Żuk highlighted that this is a Europe-wide problem.

These views have always seemed at odds with the later history of these landscapes which were so successfully exploited in the medieval and post-medieval periods. Was it so very different in prehistory or was it the very success of later agricultural regimes that had rendered the earlier occupation less visible? Was this a true reflection or were we seeing biases in the record due not just to visibility, but research interests and funding? Although the introduction of mouldboard ploughs during the Roman period has often been cited as the reason for clayland landscapes being avoided before then, does this still stand up to scrutiny?

Visibility

Many of these clayland areas are in the plough zone, with ongoing erosion of archaeological deposits while pasture, woodland, colluviation and alluviation can mask some of the evidence. Claylands are often poorly represented by prehistoric standing monuments and earthworks, which may have more to do with agricultural practices over the past 2000 years than be a true reflection of prehistoric land use. As the conference discussed, aerial reconnaissance can be successful but it is difficult to predict when and where crop marks will occur on clay substrata. The cost of aerial reconnaissance is always a factor and it is the long-term systematic vertical surveys such as have been flown for a variety of uses by Bedfordshire County Council over the past 35 years which have had the most dramatic impact. Modern image-enhancement techniques may have a role in enhancing the less-strong soil marks and crop marks typically found on clay landscapes. Similarly, geophysical survey can be a successful technique especially for locating sites from the Iron Age and later. However, artefact scatters in areas of arable cultivation are likely to be the primary evidence for prehistoric activity. Even these are not always easy to discern in clayland areas due to dispersion (Yorston *et al.* 1990) and the 'drag factor' found during ploughing and cultivation (Clark and Schofield 1991, 94).

Biases in the record

While visibility is part of the problem of detecting sites on heavier soils, other factors including research interest and funding have an effect in distorting the true picture. Biases can come in many different forms. For example, there can be a bias towards particular classes of evidence, e.g. upstanding monuments and crop marks, towards sites rather than archaeological landscapes (see below), towards particular types of site of different periods, or a bias towards particular landscape zones within given regions (Mills 1985). Many of these biases are interlinked and can be predicted to operate in regions with poorly visible archaeology, as in the case of many clayland landscapes.

Another factor which affects our perception of how a region has been exploited is the amount of fieldwork undertaken. Staged evaluation as part of the planning process following Planning Policy Guidance Note 16 (PPG16; Department of the Environment 1990) is beginning to show tangible results from clayland areas but depends on the success of curators in ensuring blank areas with few or no previous SMR entries are tested. While the Aggregates Levy Sustainability Fund is an opportunity for more fieldwork, it does concentrate on areas already well served by PPG16 – further compounding the biases. The main threat to clayland landscapes comes from ploughing and despite English Heritage's 'Ripping up the past' initiative (English Heritage 2003) an 'agricultural levy' to alleviate destruction by agricultural practices is highly unlikely in the present political climate.

Academic research has understandably concentrated on areas with more visible evidence. For the Neolithic and Bronze Age, for example, areas such as Wessex, Orkney and the Boyne Valley have been *foci* of repeated research. While these have undoubtedly been important areas, they may not necessarily have been any more special than others which have left less visible evidence. Much of their perceived status has been a result of the weight of research focused upon them (Barclay 2001).

Varieties of clay substrata

To understand how clayland areas were exploited we need to know more about the nature of clay soils. As many speakers at the conference mentioned, clayland areas show a great variety between, for example, Boulder Clay, Liassic Clays, Oxford Clays and Mercia Mudstone. Boulder Clays in particular vary greatly depending on the nature and proportion of glacial inclusions. Whereas the basic clay matrix is often very similar (Shotton 1953) the different proportion of inclusions within it do vary greatly with, for example, a very high proportion of chalk pebble flint evident from some East Midlands Boulder Clay areas (Poole *et al.* 1968, 57). In general modern clay soils are not very permeable and suffer from poor drainage (Jacks 1954, 21). Although they are usually rich in plant nutrients, poor aeration may reduce the availability of these nutrients for plants. Manure and fertilisers can help but do not have as much impact as with sandy soils. Clay soils lose structure when waterlogged due to the clay particles swelling and the soils also take longer to warm up in the spring than sandier soils (Limbrey 1975; Curtis *et al.* 1976). Clay soils do retain fertility longer than some sandy soils, however, and crops that do well include wheat, oats, barley, beans and grass.

Modern clay soils however are different from the soils confronting prehistoric communities, as they are the result of many centuries of agricultural exploitation. Woodland soils in north-west Europe tend towards the brown earth type whatever the substrata (Evans 1975, 136). The original soils developing in natural woodland would have had a friable and well-drained upper humus horizon and would have been as easy to cultivate as soils above non-clay substrata. It is following cropping or grazing, without liming or manuring, that the soil structure would have become degraded and the problems of loss of nutrients and poor drainage become apparent (Clay 2002, 3; Evans 1975, 136).

LOOKING FORWARD

Landscape survey

While the papers at the conference have outlined how much our understanding of clayland landscapes has changed over the last 25 years there is still a need for more surveys. As has been demonstrated by the papers presented, by using a variety of techniques including aerial, fieldwalking and geophysical surveys we can begin to gather evidence of how claylands in different areas have been exploited. Even basic examination of the sites and monuments record, with all their inherent biases, can show that there is more potential for occupation on clays soils than is often thought. In some cases extensive and intensive surveys can show that there has been occupation on clay substrata since the Neolithic onwards (e.g. Clay 1996; 1998; 2002; Liddle 1994; Parry 1994; 2006). An example of an intensive fieldwalking survey producing such results is from the Swift Valley in south-west Leicestershire carried out by Lutterworth Fieldwork Group (Burningham 2004; Clay 2002). This area, comprising 80% Boulder Clay, has comparable lithic densities from surface collections to that found in surveys of chalkland areas in the south of England, for example, the Vale of White Horse, Maddle Farm and East Berkshire surveys (66; Tingle 1991; Gaffney and Tingle 1989; Ford 1987). In the Swift Valley survey, six areas all with Boulder Clay substrata could be interpreted as core areas during the Neolithic and Bronze Age, while two further areas may have been procurement locations. Crop-marked sites were also present on the Boulder Clay including an elongated enclosure or long barrow (Loveday and Petchey 1982), ring ditches and several enclosures (Clay 2002, 101).

Landscape surveys are less easy to instigate at present although there is still high quality work being undertaken by the voluntary sector (Bowman and Liddle 2004; Burningham 2004) for which funding opportunities may be available. The Aggregates Levy Sustainability Fund may also be a way in which aggregate substrata (e.g. sands and gravels) could be examined in a wider context including the adjacent clay landscapes.

The planning process

It is PPG16 which has provided and will continue to provide most opportunities for examining areas of clay substrata. While often small in scale, evaluation processes in these areas can be our best opportunity of finding out how these areas are utilised.

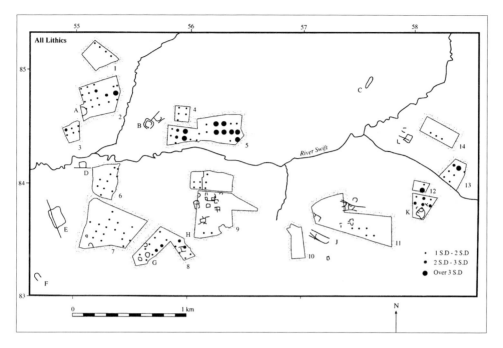

66 The Swift Valley Survey, Leicestershire, showing the distribution of all lithics by standard deviation. © *Patrick Clay 2002, fig. 30*

A good example of how this can bring tangible results is from a prehistoric clayland site found during PPG16 work at Rothley in Leicestershire in 2004. This was on a north-facing slope of Mercia Mudstone substratum – an unforgiving clay marl – in an area allocated for industrial development. There was no known archaeology from the area, air photographs were uninformative, no results were obtained from geophysical survey while fieldwalking had located a low density of flint. At this stage it could have been consigned to having no further action or a token watching brief. However, a small concentration of flint tools from fieldwalking was targeted by trial trenching. Pits and post-holes were located and were associated with flint, Peterborough Ware and Grooved Ware pottery. Subsequent excavation uncovered a Late Neolithic occupation site with a sunken-floored building within which was evidence of structured deposition including a carved stone plaque with a decoration interpreted as a stylised face (67; Cooper and Hunt 2005).

CONCLUSION

The perception of clayland exploitation is slowly changing. Prehistoric and later settlement is being discovered not only in the clay vales but also the higher Boulder Clay interfluves. While most of the examples cited during the conference are from the Later Bronze Age onwards there is some evidence that exploitation of these landscapes was also taking place during the third and second millennium BC (e.g. Albone 2000; Clay 2002).

67 Fragment of a stone plaque with incised decoration depicting a stylised face, found during excavations in 2005 on a Late Neolithic clayland site at Rothley, Leicestershire. © *Patrick Clay*

Environmental factors, such as clay substrata, are the most predictable influences when considering where people chose to live, hunt, forage, farm and in general exploit the resources of a region and predictive models have been attempted (e.g. Kvamme and Jochim 1988; Pilgrim 1987). By assuming that some locations are more suitable for settlement than others, the features determining differential suitability can be studied individually and in combination. The relative importance of different environmental variables can be assessed in predicting the location of past activities, but cannot be used to analyse more unpredictable factors in location selection. Other factors will have had different influences on this selection in the past, some of which are now impossible to measure.

Less tangible but arguably more significant factors in the activity of prehistoric groups might be described as their social knowledge of the landscape. Through their relationship with other human groups in the area, information on the qualities of a particular section of landscape can be passed on (Mithen 1990; Edmonds 1999), while knowledge of the activity of other groups within an area may also influence their actions. Similarly, historical knowledge of an area may be significant with previous sequences or events within the landscape influencing a group's responses. Positive experiences in an area might lead to an area being frequently re-visited whereas negative experiences might lead to the area being avoided. Historical knowledge might be reflected in the archaeological record where multi-period use of one location is evident. This historical knowledge of an area might also have a symbolic significance. Areas with their own 'mythology' or ritual importance might influence their interaction with different prehistoric groups. All of these factors might lead to the use, re-use or avoidance of different areas, while purely environmental factors, within which the suitability of clay soils may be an important element, should be considered in combination with these.

So, clayland archaeology is now coming of age and we are beginning to people these landscapes. The papers presented at the conference show how different techniques, often building on aerial reconnaissance, can change our perception of how these areas were used. While many of the papers suggested that these areas were being occupied from the Later Bronze Age onwards, evidence from other areas, e.g. the Swift Valley and Rothley, Leicestershire (above) has located evidence of Neolithic occupation. A holistic approach is now needed whereby clayland landscapes are considered alongside other substrata as areas which showed a variety of occupation patterns over the last 6000 years.

BIBLIOGRAPHY

Albone, J. 2000. Elmsthorpe Rise (SK 564 035). *Transactions of the Leicestershire Archaeological and Historical Society* 74, 224.

Barclay, G.J. 2001. 'Metropolitan' and 'parochial' / 'core' and 'periphery': a historiography of the Neolithic of Scotland. *Proceedings of the Prehistoric Society* 67, 1–18.

Bowman, P. & Liddle, P. (eds), 2004. *Leicestershire landscapes.* Leicestershire Museums Archaeological Fieldwork Group Monograph 1. Leicester: Leicestershire County Council.

Burningham, B. 2004. The work of two local fieldwork groups. In P. Bowman & P. Liddle (eds), *Leicestershire landscapes*, 10–11. Leicestershire Museums Archaeological Fieldwork Group Monograph 1. Leicester: Leicestershire County Council.

Clark, J.G.D. 1945. Farmers and forests in Neolithic Europe. *Antiquity* 19, 57–71.

Clark, R.H. & Schofield, A.J. 1991. By experiment and calibration: an integrated approach to archaeology of the ploughsoil. In A.J. Schofield (ed.), *Interpreting artefact scatters: contributions to ploughzone archaeology*, 93–106. Oxford: Oxbow Books.

Clay, P. 1992. An Iron Age farmstead at Grove Farm, Enderby, Leicestershire. *Transactions of the Leicestershire Archaeological and Historical Society* 66, 1–82.

Clay, P. 1996. *The exploitation of the East Midlands claylands in later Prehistory. Aspects of settlement and land-use from the Mesolithic to the Iron Age.* Unpublished PhD thesis. University of Leicester.

Clay, P. 1998. Neolithic-Earlier Bronze Age pit circles and their environs at Burley Road, Oakham, Rutland. *Proceedings of the Prehistoric Society* 64, 293–330.

Clay, P. 2002. *The East Midlands claylands in Prehistory.* University of Leicester, School of Archaeological Studies Monograph 9: Leicester.

Curtis, L.F., Courtney, F.M. & Trudgill, S. 1976. *Soils in the British Isles.* London: Longman.

Cooper, L. & Hunt, L. 2005. An engraved Neolithic plaque with Grooved Ware associations. *PAST* 50, 14–15.

Department of the Environment, 1990. *Planning and archaeology. Planning Policy Guidance Note No. 16.* London: Her Majesty's Stationery Office.

Edmonds, M. 1999. *Ancestral geographies of the Neolithic. Landscapes, monuments and memory.* London & New York: Routledge.

English Heritage, 2003. *Ripping up history. Archaeology under plough.* London: English Heritage.

Evans, J.G. 1975. *The environment of early man in the British Isles.* London: Paul Elek.

Ford, S. 1987. *East Berkshire archaeological survey*. Department of Highways and Planning, Berkshire County Council Occasional Paper 1: Reading.

Fox, C. 1932. *The personality of Britain*. Cardiff: National Museum of Wales.

Gaffney, V. & Tingle, M. 1989. *The Maddle Farm project – an integrated survey of prehistoric and rural landscapes on the Berkshire Downs*. Oxford: British Archaeological Reports.

Hall, D.N. 1985. Survey work in Eastern England. In S. Macready & F.H. Thompson (eds), *Archaeological field survey in Britain and abroad*, 25-44. London: Society of Antiquaries Occasional Paper 6.

Hoskins, W.G. 1957. *Leicestershire: an illustrated essay on the history of the landscape*. London: Hodder & Stoughton.

Jacks, G.V. 1954. *Soil*. London: Thomas Nelson.

Kvamme. K.L. & Jochim, M.A. 1988. The environmental basis of Mesolithic settlement. In C. Bonsall & J. Donald (eds), *The Mesolithic in Europe*, 1-12. Edinburgh: John Donald.

Liddle, P. 1994. The Medbourne area survey. In M. Parker Pearson & R.T. Schadla-Hall (eds), *Looking at the land. Archaeological landscapes in Eastern England: recent work and future directions*, 34-36. Leicester: Leicestershire Museums, Art Galleries and Records Service.

Limbrey, S. 1975. *Soil science in archaeology*. London: Academic Press.

Loveday, R.E. & Petchey, M. 1982. Oblong ditches: a discussion and some new evidence. *Aerial Archaeology* 8, 17-24.

Meek, J., Shore, M. & Clay, P. 2004. Iron Age enclosures at Enderby and Huncote, Leicestershire. *Transactions of the Leicestershire Archaeological and Historical Society* 78, 1–34.

Mills, N.W.T. 1985. Sample bias, regional analysis and fieldwalking in British archaeology. In C. Haselgrove, M. Millett & I. Smith (eds), *Archaeology from the ploughsoil. Studies in the collection and interpretation of field survey data*, 39-47. Sheffield: Department of Archaeology and Prehistory, University of Sheffield.

Mithen, S.J. 1990. *Thoughtful foragers: a study of prehistoric decision making*. Cambridge: Cambridge University Press.

Parry, S.J. 1994. The Raunds Area Project survey. In M. Parker Pearson & R.T. Schadla-Hall (eds), *Looking at the land. Archaeological landscapes in Eastern England: recent work and future directions*, 36-42. Leicester: Leicestershire Museums, Art Galleries and Records Service.

Parry, S.J. 2006. *The Raunds Area Survey. An archaeological study of the landscape of Raunds, Northamptonshire 1985-92*. Oxford: Oxbow Books.

Pilgrim, T. 1987. *Predicting archaeological sites from environmental variables. A mathematical model for the Sierra Nevada foothills, California*. Oxford: British Archaeological Reports (International Series) 320.

Poole, E.G., Williams, B.J. & Hains, B.A. 1968. *Geology of the country around Market Harborough*. Memoirs of the Geological Survey of Great Britain. London: Her Majesty's Stationery Office.

Shotton, F.W. 1953. The Pleistocene deposits of the area between Coventry, Rugby and Leamington and their bearing upon the topographic development of the Midlands. *Transactions of the Royal Society (Series B)* 237, 209-60.

Tingle, M. 1991. *The Vale of the White Horse survey. A study of a changing landscape in the clay lowlands of southern Britain from prehistory to the present day*. Oxford: British Archaeological Report.

Tinsley, H.M. 1981. The Bronze Age. In I.G. Simmons & M. Tooley (eds), *The environment in British Prehistory*, 210-49. London: G. Duckworth and Co. Ltd.

Turner, J. 1981. The Iron Age. In I.G. Simmons & M. Tooley (eds), *The environment in British Prehistory*, 250-81. London: G. Duckworth and Co. Ltd, London.

Woodridge, S.W. & Linton, D.H. 1933. The loam terrains of South-East England and their relation to early history. *Antiquity* 7, 297-336.

Yorston, R.M., Gaffney, V.L. & Reynolds, P.J. 1990. Simulation of artefact movement due to cultivation. *Journal of Archaeological Science* 17, 67-83.

Index